Epidauros

R. A. Tomlinson

Professor of Ancient History and Archaeology
University of Birmingham

University of Texas Press, Austin

International Standard Book Number 0–292–72044–0
Library of Congress Catalog Card Number 82–51117

Printed in Great Britain

First Edition, 1983

Contents

List of Figures

List of Plates

All the drawings were specially made for this book by Mr H. Buglass

Numerals in bold type in the text refer to the numbered buildings in Figure 5, Sanctuary of Asklepios

PART I

Introduction

The sanctuary of Asklepios at Epidauros was excavated under the auspices of the Archaeological Society of Athens, from 1881 until his death in his eightieth year in 1928 by Panayotis Kavvadias. His early excavations were comprehensively published in his two major works *Fouilles d'Epidaure*, of 1891, and, more completely Τὸ ἱερόν τοῦ Ἀσκλήπιου ἐν Ἐπιδαύρῳ of 1900. His later work was reported, more briefly (and, at the end, in summary fashion only) in the *Transactions* (Πρακτικά) *of the Archaeological Society*. There has never been a full definitive study of the sanctuary. Kavvadias' accounts and interpretation form the basis of modern popular description, the guide books on sale at Epidauros and the labelling (such as it is) in the Museum and the sanctuary itself.

Other works on the sanctuary include *Epidaure, restauration et déscription des principaux monuments du sanctuaire d'Asclépius* by Alphonse Defrasse and Henri Lechat of 1895. The restorations (the work of Defrasse) are masterpieces of the 'Beaux Arts' style, but contain too many errors and assumptions now proved erroneous to be of any value. The restoration of the circular Thymele, the most intriguing of Epidaurian buildings, was soon superseded by a better (though still incorrect) restoration made for Kavvadias and under his archaeological guidance. It is astonishing that the Defrasse version is still sold to unwitting visitors in picture-postcard form. In the 1930s F. Robert produced an exhaustive study of this building and its significance in the book *Thymélè*.

The only modern architectural studies are of the Theatre, by Armin von Gerkan and Wolfgang Müller-Wiener (published in 1961), and of several of the important buildings of the fourth and third century BC (including the temples) by G. Roux (*L'architecture de l'Argolide aux IVᵉ et IIIᵉ siècles avant JC*, also published in 1961). Roux's work forms the essential basis for any subsequent account of the buildings he discusses. More recently Roberto Patrucco has studied the Stadium (*Lo Stadio di Epidauro*, 1976). R. Martiennsen discusses the arrangement of the sanctuary and its visual planning in a chapter of his *The Idea of Space in Greek Architecture*. This contains much that is pertinent, but his argument is severely weakened by his reliance on the preliminary plan of the sanctuary in Kavvadias' *Fouilles d'Epidaure*, which mis-identifies the Propylon entrance of the large courtyard building, the Banqueting Hall, as the entrance to the sanctuary itself.

Alison Burford's discussion of the organization and administration of the construction work of the sanctuary, from the socio-historical point of view, *The Greek Temple Builders of Epidauros*, is invaluable. It is based essentially on the abundant epigraphic evidence interpreted in the light of the architectural evidence.[1] J. F. Crome gives an account of the sculptural decoration of the Temple of Asklepios (*Die Skulpturen des Asklepiostempels von Epidaurus*, 1951, a belated publication of a study carried out before the Second World War).

All these studies, understandably, concentrate on the Greek buildings from the first phase of development, the earliest structures of the late fifth century BC, and the major construction work of the fourth century which continued at least into the early part of the third. Even so there are several important buildings of this phase which have not received proper, up-to-date study; the large courtyard building, the Banqueting Hall (described by Kavvadias as the Gymnasium, and as such included in J. Delorme's general book on the Greek Gymnasium: but of this more later); the adjacent Greek Bath building (which receives a brief description in R. Ginouvès' *Balaneutikè*, but nothing more, the result more of its poor state of preservation than any lack of significance); the Hostel Building, the Katagogion, has not received more than the preliminary account of its excavation; the description of the 'palaestra' or exercise building linked to the Stadium by a vaulted passageway is even more summary, since this was one of the last buildings which Kavvadias unearthed. The various waterworks structures have not been the subject of a comprehensive study.[2]

The later structures have received much scantier attention. Roux, as it were, peels off later Roman reconstructions to get at the original fourth- and third-century buildings which are the real subject of his study, and in so doing gives a clear indication of their importance, and the thoroughness with which reconstruction work had to be carried out. Original Roman work is quite neglected; some was described by Kavvadias in his reports, but important buildings have not received the interest they deserve. Today they remain overgrown and unvisited.

This book makes no pretence to being the full and exhaustive treatment which the sanctuary so badly needs. Nevertheless, it does present a new interpretation of some monuments, along with an account of their purpose; of why the sanctuary developed, and what the cult performed there included. The understanding of this inevitably includes the Roman evidence. It is hoped that the visitor will be better equipped to disentangle the confusing visible remains, to conjure up the buildings which originally stood on these sorry foundations; and to have a fuller appreciation of what is, to the archaeologist already, one of the most fascinating places of ancient Greece.

Epidauros

The ancient Greek city state of Epidauros was situated on the northern side of the Argive peninsula. The town itself was right on the coast, that is, the Saronic Gulf, where an easily defended promontory lies adjacent to a beach. Across the gulf, Athens is about 50 km away, Corinth about 30 km, while, nearer at hand, the island of Aigina is in full view. Behind the town is a sheltered valley, now given over largely to orange groves, but beyond this the mountains soon close in, so that the area of fertile territory is not extensive, and the population can never have been large. Epidauros is certainly not one of the major cities of ancient Greece. Yet by and large the city preserved its independence in antiquity, helped partly by the rugged terrain, more by a system of alliances, which, by linking Epidauros in a friendly fashion to the infinitely more powerful state of Sparta, ensured friendly relations with Corinth, also part of the Spartan alliance, and normally counteracted the threat of any hostile activity from Argos. At times, it is true, Epidauros was attacked and her territory invaded, but none of this led to permanent occupation or loss of independence.[3]

Like Sparta, Epidauros was a Dorian state, and, despite her small size, had a social structure which to a limited extent echoed that of the major Dorian power. Her population was divided into a politically dominant section, who must certainly have lived mainly at Epidauros town, and a subservient element whose function was to farm the lands which were assigned to their superiors. These subservient inhabitants were called Dusty Feet, from the inevitable and visible consequence of their occupation. Presumably, like the helots of Sparta, they were the descendants of an earlier population which inhabited the region in the late Bronze Age.

Epidauros town, which gives its name to the city-state, was itself the site of a late Bronze Age settlement near the sea. There was another, away from the sea, controlling the small inland plain which is overlooked by Mt Kynortion; recent excavations have revealed traces of this. By the classical period this inland settlement had been dispersed, and away from the coastal region the land was more likely divided into estates. Nevertheless, the inland site continued to have some importance; a probable continuity of tradition recognized it as a place of sanctity. The cult was that of a hero, rather than a full deity, called Maleatas; his special religious competence was hunting, which in this remote area may well have been as important a source of livelihood as agriculture. His status, as a hero rather than a god, may well indicate that he was formerly a deity of the pre-Dorian

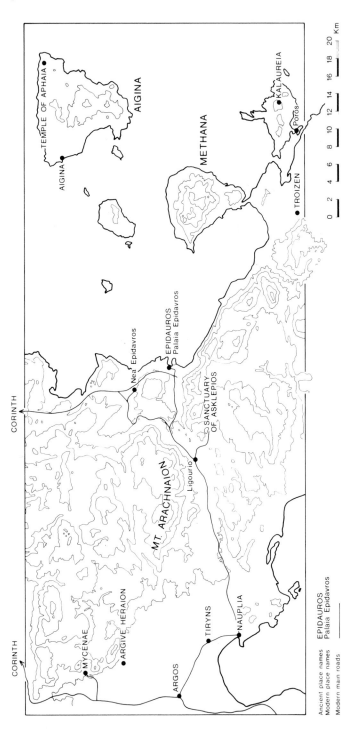

1 Map of Epidauros district

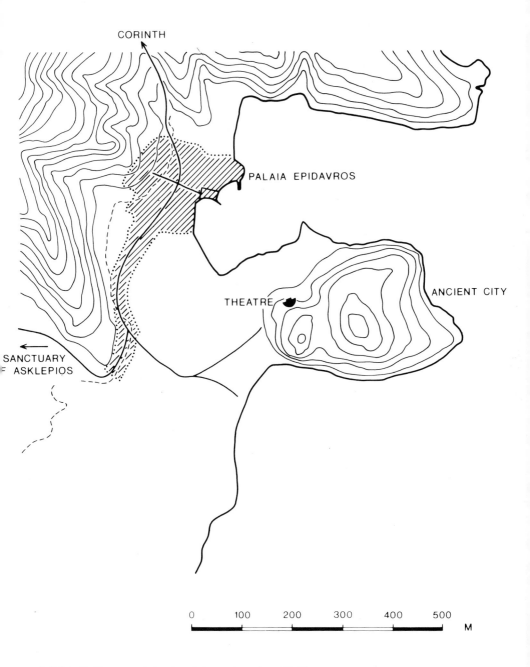

2 Palaia Epidavros and the site of the ancient city of Epidauros

1 Palaia Epidavros and the ancient city

population who had been demoted. The full god Apollo came to be established in the same sanctuary, perhaps brought there by the Dorian newcomers. Apollo assimilated Maleatas to his own cult so that the hero ceased to have any separate religious identity, becoming instead merely an epithet of Apollo, a special form of the god worshipped as 'Apollo Maleatas'.

The sanctuary was rural, and remote. The number of worshippers at any period was small, and though there are the remnants of offerings made to the god there, the early sanctuary was essentially non-architectural in form; a shrine, a sacred spot, an altar for sacrifice, but certainly not one of the splendid, new-fangled (and, probably, in origin, non-Greek) temples which gradually were adopted to house the gods of the major sanctuaries from the eighth and seventh century BC onwards. Recent excavations have discovered, under the fourth-century temple, a wall which may be part of a sixth-century predecessor.[4]   ·

The influence of Apollo extended beyond the confines of this small, hill-side sanctuary. He also came to occupy a site on the flat ground at the foot of the hill, more accessible, and certainly provided with a better water supply, but here, too, though sanctified by religious usage and cult, there was no architectural splendour, no temple, no other monumental buildings. Again, the major evidence of cult is the debris of dedicatory gifts round an altar, the earliest surviving part of which seems unlikely to have been constructed before the latter part of the sixth century BC.

There were other sanctuaries in Epidauros town, which by this time may have been more substantially built – the archaeology of the town has yet to be fully investigated, and since this would require the expropriation of valuable orange groves, with consequent heavy compensation, this is likely to remain the situation, though a restricted excavation has revealed a very well-preserved theatre, probably belonging to the third century BC.

The myth of Asklepios

There are several stories concerning the origin of Asklepios.[5] The most generally accepted (it is given in the Homeric hymn for Asklepios, in Pindar's IIIrd Pythian ode, and by Ovid in the second book of the *Metamorphoses*) is that he was the son of the god Apollo by the mortal Koronis, daughter of King Phlegyas of Trikka in Thessaly in northern Greece. Koronis was unfaithful to her divine lover; she was betrayed to Apollo by a raven and killed, either by the arrows of Apollo's sister Artemis or by Apollo himself. In remorse, the god took the unborn child from the dead mother's womb, and entrusted him to the centaur Chiron, by whom he was brought up and taught the arts of healing and hunting. In Homer's *Iliad* the two sons of Asklepios are kings of Trikka, Ithome and Oechalia, Thessalian cities.

There seems little doubt that the original legend placed the birth of Asklepios in northern Greece, in Thessaly. Messenia and, of course, Epidauros, when they became important places in the Asklepios cult, devised new versions of the legend which specifically relate Asklepios to their own locality. The way these alternative versions are reported by various ancient authors generally implies that they did not receive widespread acceptance.

As the son of a mortal woman, Asklepios was himself a mortal, not a god. He became famous as a doctor, but particularly as a doctor who could work miracles; as Apollodorus puts it, 'Having become a surgeon, and carried the craft to a high level, he not only prevented people from dying but even aroused them when they had died'. But as a mortal he died, struck by the thunderbolt of Zeus who was angry because he had revived the dead Hippolytos for personal gain. He was buried either at Kynosoura or by the river Lusios in Arcadia or at Epidauros. Subsequently he was raised to divine status; Cicero, On the Nature of the Gods, II 24, 62, says:

Human life and common custom have brought it about that men who distinguish themselves by their good deeds are raised to heaven by fame and gratitude: so Herakles, Castor and Pollux, and Asklepios.

The Epidaurian legend, according to Pausanias, said that Phlegyas, a notorious soldier, came to spy out the Peloponnese, bringing his daughter (of whose pregnancy by Apollo he was then ignorant) with him. She happened to be at Epidauros when she gave birth, and abandoned the child. There is an air of contrivance about this, almost as though the original Thessalian myth had been adapted to Epidaurian circumstances in order to justify the development there of a major centre to this cult. There is an even more determined attempt to make the whole myth an Epidaurian one in a *paian*, or hymn, inscribed on stone near the Temple of Asklepios at Epidauros by one Isyllos.[6] The first part of this refers to the establishment of a sacred procession of the 'best men' in Epidauros, organized on a tribal basis, bearing garlands of laurel to Apollo's temple, and then shoots of olive to Asklepios.

Isyllos then goes on (in verse):

Malos first built an altar of Apollo Maleatas, and enriched the sanctuary with sacrifices. Not even in Trikka of Thessaly would you try to go down into the Adyton of Asklepios, unless you first sacrificed on the holy altar of Apollo Maleatas.

Then a prose section follows, explaining how Isyllos sent Astylaidas to Delphi to ask whether he should inscribe on stone the *paian* he had composed. He received a favourable response. So the *paian* follows. In this he gives his version of the birth of Asklepios:

Zeus gave the Muse Erato to Malos as his bride. Phlegyas *who dwelt in Epidauros* married the daughter of Malos and Erato, Kleophema, and had by her a daughter Aigle, called Koronis because of her beauty. She was seduced by Apollo, and bore a child in the sanctuary. Apollo called the child Asklepios, from the mother's name Aigle.

Isyllos gives himself away with his reference to Trikka, entirely gratuitous unless he felt he had to stress Epidauros' priority of claim. Malos and Maleatas were known at Epidauros to have been strictly and locally connected; the point argued is that even Trikka yields priority to Maleatas, and so, by implication, to Epidauros in the Asklepios cult. In the *paian* the legend is even more directly shifted than in Pausanias' account of the Epidaurian version. Phlegyas now *dwells* in Epidauros; the child is born in the sanctuary. It is, perhaps, wrong to accuse Isyllos of deliberate distortion; but one has to accept that he has been carried away by his enthusiastic support for his own sanctuary.

We cannot even be sure that the connection developed out of the supposed burial of Asklepios at Epidauros. The evidence that his tomb was there is late, and certainly post-dates the great development of the sanctuary (where the existence of a tomb must be related to the developed architecture). Again, the honour is disputed with other places. Cicero, indeed, finds the whole problem so insoluble that he postulated three distinct Asklepii.

Though the worship of Asklepios as a god can be seen to be spreading in the Greek world from the late fifth century BC onwards, eventually to be established as far afield as Cilicia, the earliest development of his cult is totally obscure. There are two real possibilities. The first is that he was originally a god, perhaps of very restricted significance who 'decayed', like Maleatas, to a lower status before experiencing a revival of religious fortune. The alternative, obviously, is that he was a real man, living at a fairly remote period, whose achievements came to acquire a reputation analogous to those of a god, and led eventually to his assimilation to full divine status. Both arguments have their supporters, and both are possible, given the general way in which Greek religion and religious ideas develop. The concept of Asklepios as a mortal seems inextricably linked with Thessaly, and Trikka in particular, but this does not satisfactorily explain his arrival at Epidauros. It would be useful if we could determine when this happened, but this is impossible. He must have been there in the early fifth century BC when his name was inscribed on a dedicatory offering by one Mikylos, which was found under Building E (see plan 4) in the main sanctuary. There is no earlier evidence for him; but on the other hand there is no earlier evidence for Apollo either, except the presumption that the upper sanctuary was his (rather than one shared with Asklepios); and since it clearly was a sanctuary at a significantly earlier period, Apollo was already there. As Asklepios was acknowledged to be Apollo's son even as a human there is no difficulty in associating him with the cult of his father, even if this did not necessarily happen in the upper sanctuary. The development of the lower sanctuary, in its primitive and entirely unmonumental form, may already have stressed the healing aspect; the easier accessibility, the abundant water supplies available there make it more suited to this purpose. While Apollo was worshipped in the upper sanctuary in other aspects – hunting in particular – in the lower as a god of healing it would be appropriate from the start that his doctor son was associated with him; whether or not as a god rather than a hero is more than we can say of the original development, but there is little reason to doubt that Asklepios had divine status by the end of the sixth century, and may have enjoyed it, if only in a purely local context, longer than that.

The cult

The forms of ritual devoted to the cult of any Greek god were varied; Asklepios is no exception to this pattern. Each state had its own calendar of sacred occasions. The most important of these were the festivals: each god had at least one, many had several (though in this case one festival would have supreme importance). Festivals were, normally, annual events with perhaps a special effort every fourth year. They were great public occasions, the central act of which was the performance of an appropriate sacrifice at an open air altar in full view of the participating crowds. In addition to these great public occasions, there was, it seems, an incessant sequence of smaller religious acts. These are of two categories, sacrifices or other acts performed on behalf of the community by specially designated priests, without the attendance of the populace; and private sacrifices performed by individuals in their own interests. Again, Asklepios conforms to this pattern.

Public cult: The festival of Asklepios at Epidauros was celebrated nine days after the festival of Poseidon at the Isthmus of Corinth, the Isthmian Games, which, it appears, were probably held towards the end of April. By the fourth century it was attended by worshippers from all over Greece, and since it included contests it was an obvious economy if those who had participated in the festival at Isthmia could then make their way over to Epidauros before returning home. All Greek communities were invited to name special representatives who were responsible for the reception of the Asklepios cult in their own cities; cities with which the Epidaurians had close and friendly relations could send representatives to participate in the official aspect of the festival, but in addition ordinary worshippers would be welcome. They gathered first at Epidauros town, and then made their way in a sacred, formal procession to the sanctuary, bringing with them the animals for sacrifice. On the journey they chanted hymns of praise to Asklepios, which were called *paians*; that is, they took their name from the hymn sung to Apollo, from whose cult the idea was doubtless adapted for his son. The most famous of these, sung by the Athenians at their festival of Asklepios, was by the tragedian Sophocles (who was one of the people involved in the acceptance of Asklepios and his cult at Athens), but only a fragment of this has survived. From Epidauros itself we have the complete text of the *paian* of Isyllos, mentioned above, which he composed (so the inscription on which it is recorded says) in honour of Apollo and Asklepios (the date of the inscription is about 300 BC):

People, praise the god of the Paian, dwellers in this holy Epidauros. For thus the word came to the ears of our ancestors, O Phoibos Apollo. Father Zeus is said to have given the muse Erato to Malos as his bride in holy matrimony. Phlegyas, who dwelt in Epidauros as fatherland, married the daughter of Malos whom Erato, her mother, bore; she was called Koronis. Seeing her in the house of Malos Phoibos of the golden bow ended her virginity. You went into her beautiful bed, golden-haired son of Lato. I worship you. In the perfumed sanctuary Aigle bore a child; and the son of Zeus, together with the Fates, and Lachesis, the noble midwife, freed her from the birth pangs. Apollo named him Asklepios from the name of his mother, Aigle; he is he who ends illness, the giver of health, the great gift for mortals, Ie paian, Ie paian, hail Asklepios; increase Epidauros, your mother city, send bright health to our minds and bodies. Ie paian, Ie paian.

The poetry is atrocious (the dozen or so words of Sophocles' *paian* which have survived not surprisingly show a more marked poetic achievement). The myth is tendentious, giving a fictitious prominence to the role of Epidauros. This is the Epidaurian viewpoint; so the procession gave a boost to Epidauros' claims, not just praise to Asklepios.

On entering the sanctuary, and at the performance of various elements in the ritual, a solemn purification by washing would be necessary. Just inside the Propylon is a well, one of the oldest constructions of the sanctuary; elsewhere several shallow circular basins, designed for ritual washing, have been found, often bearing inscriptions indicating their dedication to Asklepios or one of the other gods of the sanctuary, as it were as part of the sacred furniture. They were almost certainly given by the *hiaromnamones*, state officials who administered the cult, presumably in celebration of their year of office.[7] The cleanliness was not merely physical. According to Porphyrius there was an inscription at Epidauros: 'He who enters the fragrant temple must be pure; purity is to think holy thoughts'; washing should be regarded as a symbol of purity.

The exact sequence of events at the festival is uncertain. The sacrifices are defined in an inscription of about 400 BC[8] (that is, before the major architectural development). This is in fact a double text; the first part recording sacrifice to Apollo, the second, in almost identical terms, to Asklepios.

[To sacrifice to Apollo a bull; and a bull to the gods who have the same temple] To sacrifice these on the a[ltar] of Apollo and a cock to Leto, and another to Artemis. The portion for the god: a *medimnus* (measure) of barley, half a *medimnus* of wheat, a twelfth part of wine, and the leg of the first bull. Let the *hiaromnamones* take the second leg. Of the second bull, let them give one leg to the singers, and the other to the guards, and the entrails.

To sacrifice to Asklepios a bull, and a bull to the gods who have the same temple, and a cow to the goddesses who have the same temple. To sacrifice these on the altar of Asklepios, and a cock. Let them dedicate as the portion for Asklepios a *medimnus* of barley, half a *medimnus* of wheat, a twelfth part of wine. Let them set aside one leg of the first bull to the god, and let the *hiaromnamones* take the second leg. Of the second bull [let them give] [a leg] to the singers and the other [to the guards, and the entrails].

These represent, probably, official sacrifices on behalf of the city, since the parts of the bulls which are not burnt for the god are given to the city officials, the *hiaromnamones*. It is not to be supposed that these were the only offerings; others might come from other cities and from individuals. (For other cities there is clear evidence in another Epidaurian inscription[9] which also refers to participation in the procession:

God, Good Fortune. It was decided by the Epidaurians; the Astypalaians, being colonists and benefactors of the Epidaurians are to have exemption from tax, and right of asylum in peace and war, and by land and sea. The sacrificial victims of the Astypalaians are to go in the procession of the Epidaurians. They are to sacrifice to the gods in Epidauros.)

What rules governed the distribution of these is totally uncertain, but Pausanias[10] tells us the meat had to be consumed within the sanctuary, and it would be surprising if there was not enough to provide for the thousands who attended. Other types of sacrifice might be made, but there was a prohibition on the sacrifice of goats; the Epidaurian legend was that when the infant Asklepios had been abandoned on Mt Tithion by his mother, he was suckled by one of the she goats that grazed that mountain, but there was a similar prohibition at other sanctuaries where the Epidaurian version of the birth legend would not have been accepted.

A formal banquet was included in the ritual, and in the developed sanctuary there was a building which served as a Banqueting Hall for select worshippers, containing several rooms of varying size arranged round a large central courtyard. It has a magnificent entrance Propylon, complete with a ramped approach which shows that the worshippers entered in solemn procession. This must surely have included the recipients of the official sacrifice, the *hiaromnamones*, the bards, and, probably, the guards. The dining-rooms in this building are either for select groups of eleven, or larger groups, up to say a hundred or so, and thus appear to mark the distinction between the important *hiaromnamones* and the others. It is not at all unlikely that the courtyard of this building was the place where the bards performed their sacred odes, for a special auditorium, or *odeion*, was built here in the second century AD. There are references, concerned with the Asklepios cult elsewhere, to the sacred table on which food for the god was placed as though at a banquet; so the god also participated in the banquet enjoyed by his human worshippers. At Syracuse the table was golden, and apparently placed in a context where the humans dined. There must have been such a table at Epidauros also, either in the Temple or in the Banqueting Hall where an alcove in the north wall is a likely place for it.

Another important part of the festival was the contest. There were two parts to this, athletic and artistic. There is evidence for the athletic contest early in the fifth century BC. Pindar's Vth Nemean ode records a victory of Themistios in the *pankration* (all-in wrestling) at Epidauros. The evidence for artistic contests is a century or so later, in Plato's dialogue, the *Ion*[11] where Ion explains that the Epidaurians worship the god with a contest of rhapsodes, and of 'other music'. The important thing here is that the evidence for these aspects of the cult antedates the great architectural development of the sanctuary; the buildings were created to improve the facilities for something which already existed and was an essential part of the religious practice associated with Asklepios.

Private cult: None of these aspects of public cult is in any way peculiar to Asklepios, and this ritual (whatever the precise details) must have been similar in broad terms to that devoted to any other god. Asklepios' peculiar importance rests with the private cult; that is, the religious activity undertaken in the sanctuary by individuals for their personal well-being, and in particular the healing of illness.

This aspect was not restricted to the period of the festival (though there is no reason to suppose that it was excluded at that time). With the growth in popularity of the cult, the numbers resorting to Asklepios for miraculous cures no doubt increased out of all proportion; and it is doubtless this which made possible, and necessary, the great architectural development of the sanctuary in the fourth century BC, even though the greater part of this development was concerned with the public rather than the private aspects of cult.

Each individual had to approach the god by way of a set ritual. This included preliminary sacrifice and purification by ritual bathing. The general method of approach was for the suppliant to spend a night sleeping in the sanctuary, a special building, the Abaton (the Unapproachable building – unapproachable, that is, to those who had not performed the necessary preliminaries) being provided for this purpose. While the suppliant was asleep the god manifested himself, generally in the form of a vision, which the suppliant subsequently remembered. Alternatively the suppliant might be approached by a sacred snake. Numerous cures were recorded on inscriptions which have survived; six of the slabs on which they were written were still standing when Pausanias visited the sanctuary in the second century AD. Four slabs were found by the excavators; two are virtually intact, one is only a small fragment.[12] They date from the fourth century, from the great period of development at the sanctuary. The narrative is succinct, and to the point, but gives an excellent impression of the psychological impact.

> A dumb boy. He came to the sanctuary concerning his voice. When he had performed the preliminary sacrifice, and completed the accustomed ritual, after this the servant who brings the fire for the god, looking at the boy's father asked him to promise to make the thank offering sacrifice for the cure within the year, if he got what he had come for. The boy suddenly said 'I promise'. His father was amazed and asked him to say it again..The boy said it again, and after this was healthy.

Here, obviously, the cure was effected without the need to spend the night in the Abaton, the incubation ritual.

> Euhippos carried a spear-head in his jaw for six years. When he had gone to sleep the god extracted the spear-head and put it in his hand. When day came Euhippos went away cured, with the spear-head in his hands.

> Hagestratos had head pains. He suffered from continuous sleeplessness because of the pains in his head. When he came to the Abaton, he slept, and saw a vision in a dream. It appeared to him that the god cured the pain in his head, made him stand up naked, and taught him the lunge used in pankration wrestling. When day came he went away healthy, and not long after won the pankration at Nemea.

> A man had his toe cured by a serpent. This man suffered terribly from a malignant ulcer on a toe. During the day he was taken outside by the attendants and settled on a seat. He was seized by sleep. Meanwhile a snake came out of the Abaton and cured the toe with its tongue. Having done this it returned to the Abaton. The man woke up cured, and said he saw a vision; it seemed that a handsome youth had put a drug on his toe.

Not all the cures required sleep or visions, nor were the snakes (which, to judge from this last cure, were real, not just seen in visions) the only temple creatures concerned with the cures:

> Lyson of Hermione, a blind boy. While awake his eyes were healed by one of the sanctuary dogs, and he went away cured.

> A dog cured a boy from Aigina. He had a growth on his neck. When he came to the god one of the sacred dogs cured him with his tongue while he was awake, and made him healthy.

Sacred dogs: there was an alternative version of the Asklepios myth, which said that when the infant Asklepios was abandoned on the mountain he was suckled by a dog. The existence of 'sacred' dogs, living in the sanctuary, may be the result of this.

Sometimes Asklepios' help was directed to more practical, and certainly non-medical, matters:

When Kallikrateia's husband died, she knew that gold had been concealed by her husband, but she could not find it when she looked for it. So she came to the sanctuary about the treasure, and when she was asleep she saw a vision. It seemed that the god stood by her and said that in the month of Thargelion the gold lay inside a lion at mid-day. When it was day she left, and having returned home, first of all she looked at the head of the stone lion – there was a tomb near her house, with a stone lion placed on it. When she didn't find the treasure, a priest explained to her that the god did not mean that the treasure was in the stone head, but in the shadow cast by the lion at mid-day in the month of Thargelion. Afterwards she made a search for the gold in this way, and found the treasure.

The survival of these lists is the result of chance, and it is clear that much similar information has been lost. Nevertheless, we are entitled to treat the surviving inscriptions as a typical random sample of the people who resorted to Asklepios during the fourth century BC. There is a slight preponderance of men to women, but not enough to be of any great significance: both men and women equally had access to Asklepios and his cures. When their home cities are named they are more often in the vicinity of Epidauros (four from Epidauros itself, three from Troizen, three from Halieis). Others came from further afield in the Peloponnese, the Saronic Gulf, and more distant parts of the Greek world – Lampsakos, Thasos, Knidos, for example. The quality of the people concerned is less easy to determine. Some are children brought by their parents. One – a baggage carrier taking vases to the sanctuary for his master – was probably a slave (but the 'cure' was the miraculous repair of the vase, not of a slave as suppliant). Amphimnastos was an itinerant fishmonger, not a prestigious occupation, who tried to cheat the god, and was punished by him. Euhippos was presumably wounded in battle as a soldier, which might mean he was a citizen with certain property qualifications but in the fourth century one cannot be certain of this. Otherwise there are no indications of status (except that several of the women are married) or occupation. Some people chose to remain anonymous.

In all probability, the recording of the miraculous cure in these inscriptions is not the result merely of spontaneous gratitude. In the event of a cure there was an obligation to the patient to fulfil thank offering sacrifices, and one gets the impression that the priests of the cult welcomed the publicity these testimonials provided, much in the same way that Roman Catholics acknowledge benefits received by divine or saintly intervention in the personal columns of newspapers.

The history of the sanctuary

To the Greeks every aspect of human life and experience was watched over by a particular deity. Each city had its own patron god whose special concern was to see to its well-being. The origins of these religious beliefs belong to the remote, prehistoric past, and were largely long-established by the time the Greeks began to make written records of their actions and achievements. Nevertheless, the system was not static. Changes in the human situation caused changes in the superhuman; old cults, concerned with an obsolete way of life, naturally decayed; new cults might be introduced to accommodate changed circumstances.

The patron deity of Epidauros was probably Apollo but no clear record survives, and there is no archaeological or other evidence from the city itself. The sanctuary where his cult was assimilated to that of Maleatas was some distance to the south, away from the city. In some Greek cities the principal sanctuary of the protecting deity is located at a distance from the town – particularly where the sacred spot appears to have a sanctity dating back to the Bronze Age. This could well apply here; but the sanctuary is so poor, so ill-equipped, that it hardly seems adequate even for an admittedly small city like Epidauros. It is more likely that the chief sanctuary was at Epidauros town.

By the Roman period, Pausanias could write that the whole land of Epidauros was specially sacred to Asklepios. The rural sanctuary had developed an architectural splendour, but it was for the sake of Asklepios rather than his father Apollo (though Apollo was still worshipped there, and certainly benefited from the much greater attention the sanctuary now received). But Asklepios was nevertheless a relative newcomer, certainly to divine status. If his worship as a god developed only in the fifth century BC, Epidauros would have needed another protector before that time. It is, in fact, doubtful whether Asklepios did become the protecting deity. Some inscriptions relating to public matters not involving his cult have been found in the sanctuary, and it is usual for these types of inscriptions to be set up in the sanctuary of the protecting deity of the city. But there are not many of these inscriptions; and other sanctuaries could be used, so that this does not demonstrate a particular role for Asklepios. What is quite clear is that in international terms Epidauros was famous for the sanctuary of Asklepios (indeed, it was the city's only claim to international status, a fact of which the Epidaurians were doubtless well aware when they promoted the cult).

The archaeological evidence[13] points to the existence of the Maleatas sanctuary on its hill from the eighth century BC onwards; this is the period when many Greek sanctuaries seem to have developed. The cult in this particular sanctuary is later attested as that of Apollo, under the epithet Maleatas; whether there were other cults at this early date is quite unclear, but the fourth-century inscription which describes the offering to be made to Apollo, as we have seen (page 17), refers to the other gods who dwell in the same sanctuary, and, significantly, Lato his mother and Artemis his sister. Asklepios, however, has his offerings defined in a similar, but separate decree. There is no question but that this earliest sanctuary was entirely unsophisticated in architectural terms.

The earliest documentary evidence for the establishment of the cult of Asklepios at Epidauros comprises dedicatory offerings made to him and found by Kavvadias in the excavation of Building E. These were associated with ash and other debris representing the residue of sacrifice, and belonging to the period before the construction of that building. They probably came from the nearby altar and its vicinity. There are two early inscriptions amongst these; one on a bronze *patera* (or shallow offering bowl) records its dedication to Asklepios by one Mikylos, and is written in an early form of the Argive Greek alphabet; the other, on a bronze vase, announces that it is the property of Pythian Apollo. Kavvadias believed that the inscriptions belonged to the sixth century BC and on the basis of this it is usually stated that the Asklepios cult was established at Epidauros in the sixth century.[14]

More recently, in her study of the early local Greek alphabets, Lilian Jeffrey[15] has come to the conclusion that the Asklepios *patera* is 'hardly earlier than *c*. 500'; this means that we can be sure only that the cult was established by the early fifth century; it may have been there earlier, but if so, and for how long, we cannot tell.

Development of the sanctuary and cult during the fifth century was slow. Epidauros, exposed to the political rivalries of Athens and Sparta, was not in a position to prosper, nor was there any particular reason why her cults should attract additional attention. The sanctuary of Asklepios therefore remained essentially unsophisticated. There was no temple, in the developed architectural sense. The sanctuary contained an altar, at which sacrifices to Apollo were made; there may have been a separate altar to Asklepios but there is no certain evidence for it. There was a well by the side of the road leading into the sanctuary from Epidauros town, which may have provided the water needed for the ritual purification of those entering the precinct of the god. There was probably another sacred well, which was used for the processes of effecting cures. There may have been some simple buildings, of no architectural pretensions, but nothing more. Doubtless there were also votive offerings; but these in general would have been vases, whether of terracotta or metal. There may have been statues, and there may have been altars to other deities, but, again, firm evidence is lacking.

The impetus for the development of the cult is almost certainly the plague which devastated Athens in the early part of the Peloponnesian War, in 430 BC. Though the plague was particularly virulent at Athens, where the conditions caused by the evacuation of the rural population within the protection of the walls were particularly suited to an epidemic, it frightened the whole of Greece, and certainly affected other regions. Epidauros was attacked by an Athenian force while the plague was raging in Athens. Elsewhere, Athenian expeditions brought the plague with them. If Epidauros was not affected, or affected only lightly, her people would have had every reason to be grateful to the healing god.

The promotion of the cult was almost certainly due to dedicated individuals who took upon themselves the duty of spreading the worship of the new god. As far as one can tell, they did this because of firmly held convictions that the worship of Asklepios, in addition to that of the established gods, was essential to the well-being of any Greek community. There was no 'conversion' to the religion of Asklepios, to the exclusion of all else. The established gods and cults would not be disturbed or displaced in any way – this would be recognized as harmful – but the community had to be convinced that it needed Asklepios as well. The process can be seen at Athens where an inscription[16] records the introduction of Asklepios in 420 BC by an Athenian supporter called Telemachos.

By the fifth century medicine in Greece had developed along scientific lines: the observation of symptoms, the deduction of the nature of the disease from the symptoms, and the application of appropriate remedies, including drugs. In this it was, of course, the remedy, or the proper application of the remedy, which effected the cure. It is most unlikely that this system ever completely supplanted or replaced belief in supernatural cures (which still exists even in Western society where belief in the supernatural, and the powers of the supernatural in general, have been supplanted by rational material-ism). The power of the gods, and the hold which they possessed – and used – over all human affairs, cannot but have affected matters of health as well. The growth of the Asklepios cult was not, then, a new aspect of Greek religion, but rather the concentration of a particular aspect – healing – on the particular personality – Asklepios. However scientific the practice of Greek doctors had become it was inevitably deficient. The real causes of disease were often not known, and, without microscopes, undiscoverable. Surgery, without anaesthetics, was painful and desperate. There were abundant circumstances in which human medicine was bound to fail, and where the only hope was to invoke the power of the gods. In the conditions of late fifth-century

Greece (and the inability of the Athenians to help the victims of the plague demonstrated this), it is not surprising that the cult of Asklepios rapidly gained importance. It was at about this time that the first important architectural development of the sanctuary at Epidauros took place. This was the construction of the building labelled 'E' by Kavvadias.

The major development belongs to the fourth century BC, when the sanctuary clearly took on an international status, and received buildings worthy of comparison with those in other major Greek sanctuaries. Its international importance, which is in such marked contrast to its position in the preceding century, is attested by an inscription[17] originally set up in the sanctuary around 365 BC. This lists the *Theorodokoi*, that is, individuals in other Greek cities who received and otherwise supported ambassadors (*theoroi*) sent out by Epidauros to promote the cult and to collect funds for the improvement of the sanctuary. This was a normal procedure; the sanctuary of Apollo at Delphi benefited in the same way, though obviously the response depended on the importance of the cult. That the Epidaurians could now do this for Asklepios is in itself evidence of the status his cult had achieved. This list is not complete; there are no names recorded for any of the Peloponnesian towns or for the Aegean islands. It is unlikely they were omitted, and so presumably were recorded on another stone which has not survived. What survives records names for central and northern Greece (Megara, Athens, the Boeotian cities), Thessaly, Greek cities in Macedonia, the Macedonians (represented by their king, Perdikkas, indicating that the inscription belongs to his brief reign which lasted from 365 to 359 BC); the Greek cities of Thrace, the north-western Greeks, and then the Greeks of Sicily and Italy.

Despite this international support, the administration of the sanctuary and its affairs remained in Epidaurian hands.[18] A board of financial officials, the *hiaromnamones*, four in number, together with the priest of Asklepios, was responsible for the financial and other control of the construction programme; presumably it also supervised the general running of its religious functions. Most particularly the board was responsible for organizing, in all aspects, the physical development of the sanctuary, the construction of the buildings which were obviously intended to enhance its status so it could accept comparison with other major sanctuaries whose international reputation was of longer standing and whose financial support from outside was greater.

Fortunately (and following a precedent set by those responsible for the construction of temples and other buildings in Athens in the previous century) the *hiaromnamones* were punctilious in recording on stone the necessary business arrangements for the development of the sanctuary of Asklepios. Many of these inscriptions have survived.[19] The construction even of individual buildings in the sanctuary was not entrusted to a single person, whether architect or building contractor, with overall responsibility to see that the work was done properly. This responsibility belonged to the *hiaromnamones* and the inscriptions were vital to their successful performance of this function. They contracted out the work in clearly defined parts: the quarrying and transport of stone, the working of stone, the construction of different parts of the building, the different aspects of embellishment, and so on. The contractors came from various parts of Greece, not necessarily from Epidauros itself, so that they were not themselves automatically subject to Epidaurian legal control. To avoid the difficulties that this might cause, the *hiaromnamones* insisted that the work of each contractor should be covered by a financial surety, put up by guarantors who were of Epidaurian citizenship and therefore subject to Epidaurian legal control; it was thus in the interests of the guarantor to make personal arrangements with the constructor that would minimize his risk before accepting the intermediary role (though possibly some guarantors were influenced in accepting more of a risk by piety to Asklepios). Obviously, in this situation it was necessary to have an unequivocal, publicly accessible record of the contract in all its financial details, and an inscription erected in the sanctuary itself was the best method of achieving this, as it had been in Athens in the fifth century.

Thus, although the inscriptions are legal and financial rather than architectural documents, and are not in any sense fully descriptive specifications, they do shed light on architectural matters: the sequence of construction (and so, in general terms, the chronology of the development), the cost of the building. They tell us something of the individuals concerned, and they help with the interpretation of the ruined remains, and, at times, the reconstruction of elements which have been totally destroyed. They are particularly important because they comprise the most complete series (although not intact) of such building documents to have survived from the ancient world, and because they happen to refer to a development which was concentrated into a relatively restricted period.

None of the inscriptions includes a precise and unequivocal statement of its date, though they may contain incidental evidence which helps elucidate the sequence of building. Particularly important here are the inscriptions referring to the circular Thymele which make it clear that work on this building began after the completion of the

Temple (which was finished in the space of four years and eight months) and was spread out over a period of not less than twenty-seven years. It is more difficult to interpret this information in terms of precise calendar years. The architectural evidence, of style and form, of the Temple clearly indicates a date in the first half of the fourth century BC and, with every degree of certainty, between 390 (that is, a short time after the conclusion of the Peloponnesian War) and 370. Stylistic criteria alone make it difficult to be more precise than this. The inscriptions do not give any more precise information. Recent suggestions[20] that economic considerations indicate a date about 375–370 have found a measure of acceptance. The problem is that at this time the Greek world, after a period of stability harshly enforced by the Spartans with Persian backing, was once more slipping into war. From the winter of 379 to 378, when the Spartan garrison was expelled from Thebes in Boeotia, to the battle of Leuktra in 371, and with only one very brief interlude, Sparta and Boeotia were at war; though Epidauros must have been involved only marginally, the conflict may have disrupted the flow of funds. It could, of course, be argued that work would not have started until sufficient funds had been accumulated, and the rapid construction of the Temple suggests that that was so. It may even be that the initial funds were collected in the Peloponnese, and that the later inscription recording the collection of funds in the rest of the Greek world was possible only after Leuktra had settled the dispute between Sparta and Thebes in Thebes' favour. But if we are to argue solely on a suitable historical context, the period between 387 (the enforced peace) and 378 is the best time, at least for the decision to collect funds for the start of the radical reconstruction of the sanctuary.

It is difficult to say how extensive were the original plans, and the inscriptions shed no direct light on this. There is a distinct architectural coherence to the sanctuary, which suggests a single, concerted plan, but in a sense this is belied by the obvious length of time taken over the construction; work was still in progress in the third century. It is probably best to suppose that when work started there was at least a general idea of what should be done, and that this remained a guiding theme throughout. Moreover, there seems to have developed a continuity of building tradition in all aspects: design, details, the types of stone and other material employed and particularly (the inscriptions support this) the actual craftsmen. At the same time, there can be little doubt that when work started those responsible had no idea how long it would take, but merely authorized that construction for which funds were available. If this were so, the sequence of construction (where it can be established) should serve to demonstrate the relative importance to the cult and its worshippers of the various buildings in the sanctuary.

There is no doubt that, as one would expect, the Temple came first. Whether the long altar already existed is uncertain; but even though it is not exactly aligned with the Temple, the two are closely related. Obviously, to compare with the other major sanctuaries it was essential for Asklepios to be provided with a full and imposing temple, and the priority afforded it is natural. The relevant inscription[21] was found some 20 m east of the Temple. The accounts cover the entire period of construction. The entry for each year (except the first) begins with the annual payment of the salary for the architect Theodotos. He gets 353 drachmas a year; hardly a munificent wage and no more than was paid to a craftsman; for this he not only undertakes the design but supervises the entire construction. In general the inscription gives a precise impression of the progress made in construction. The first entry records the contract for the quarrying, transport and assembly of stone for the foundations of the peristasis (placed with Mnasicles of Epidauros); the second entry, the contract for quarrying and transport of stone for the peristyle, is placed with Lykios of Corinth, since here the superior Corinthian limestone was required for the visible part of the Temple. By the side of each main column of the inscription is a second column recording minor payments; included amongst these are payments to heralds, who are dispatched to various places in connection with the construction of the Temple. In the second year, contracts placed include one for the blocks of the paving and the entrance ramp, and another for getting them in place. In the third year ivory is to be provided for the decoration of the door and the walls are to be polished; we know also about the placing of contracts for the carving of the decorative sculpture. Few contracts are placed in the fourth year (which serves to remind us that work was not necessarily completed in the year in which the contract was placed). At the end of the fourth year it was anticipated that work would take only another half year so Theodotos was given only half his annual salary. A final payment of 70 drachmas was probably made to him (the name is not completely legible) suggesting that, in fact, work continued for yet another two months. Most of the inscription is taken up with contracts and payments, but there are occasional records of receipts (surprisingly, towards the end, in the fourth year), from two individuals Euboulos and Hagemon; and from the city of Hermione the sum of 1241½ Aiginetan drachmas, a figure which reads very much like the result of a collection taken on behalf of the Temple fund. The accounts for the gold and ivory statue of Asklepios, far less well preserved, were inscribed on a second stone.[22]

The next important building in the sequence was the circular Thymele. The inscription for this[23] is substantially preserved, but not as completely as that giving the accounts for the Temple, and there are considerable gaps. The beginning is missing, and though the material ordered and worked is such that it obviously belongs to the Thymele, this is first directly stated in the second part where we are told the accounts are those of the makers of the Thymele. The first part of the inscription seems, from the recurrence of certain names and the style of the lettering, to be very close to the inscription for the Temple, and it is logical to conclude that work began on the Thymele immediately after the Temple was complete; however it is clear from the distinct entries for each year that, unlike the Temple, work on the Thymele was very protracted. It is not certain exactly how many years' accounts are lost in the gap of about 128 lines in the first part of the inscription; probably about six but the surviving text definitely covers 22 separate and distinct years. In all, the Thymele must have taken around 30 years to build. In some years, the 17th (conventionally assuming six years in the missing part of the accounts), 24th, 25th and 26th, no expenses are recorded, so presumably no work was done. In other years expenses were small (29 drachmas 2 obols in year 16, 13 drachmas 4½ obols in year 22, 55 drachmas in year 23). It looks very much as though the pace of the work was dictated by the availability of funds though other causes of delay are possible. In addition, there is an original break in the text (a space for three lines deliberately left empty) between the first and second parts, and this may indicate an interlude. In these circumstances it is precarious to assign precise dates; but the years between 360 and 330 are the most likely time for the building of this monument.

The Thymele inscription introduces to the Epidaurian texts a new style in which letters of each line are arranged in columns, as it were, immediately beneath the letters of the preceding line, and above these of the next line – the 'stoichedon style'. This style seems to continue to the end of the fourth century, and is used for inscriptions relating to the next sequence of structures. These include an unidentified temple, another temple, probably that of Artemis (perhaps of about 330–320 BC), the Epidoteion, the Theatre, probably the Stadium, and a Hostel building.

A final group of inscriptions continues the development into the first part of the third century BC. Many of these refer to utilitarian residential buildings, some of them on Mt Kynortion. There are other buildings, some of them important, which are not mentioned in the surviving inscriptions. These include the Propylon and, almost certainly, the great courtyard building which served as a Banqueting Hall. The absence of inscriptions (or the impossibility of relating to these buildings certain inscriptions so badly preserved that it is not clear to which buildings they refer) is again unfortunate, but must be purely the result of the chances of survival. One thing is absolutely certain: these buildings also were put up in this great phase of construction, the Propylon and the Banqueting Hall probably quite late in the sequence.

There are no building inscriptions of a later period. During the period of about a century to which the inscriptions belong, the sanctuary of Asklepios had been transformed from its humble origins to its definitive arrangement. It now had all the buildings necessary for the full and convenient performance of all aspects, public and private, of the healing cult. Moreover, though not the largest, or most spectacular or (certainly) the most expensively constructed, the buildings were adequate not only for their function but also for the appropriate glorification of Asklepios.

Thereafter the fortunes of the sanctuary depend on the fortunes of Greece. After the early part of the third century BC it is unlikely that there were sufficient funds for any lavish embellishment, and little impetus to replace structures which were adequate for their purpose. Dedicatory offerings were made by the *hiaromnamones* and others, and a number of inscribed bases on which these stood have survived. As far as these can be dated (usually only by letter-style), they seem to belong to the fourth and third centuries, rather than the second. The same is true of the long inscriptions recording the cures effected by Asklepios. Another category of inscription seems to belong essentially to the period from the end of the third century BC, when it became the custom to record the names of manumitted slaves on the seats of the Stadium, though this does not imply that the seats were provided at this period at the expense of the slave owners or the manumitted slaves; similar manumissions are recorded on already existing buildings and structures at other sanctuaries, such as Delphi.

During the third century Epidauros received the support of the kings of Macedon, and the Epidaurians showed their gratitude by erecting statues in their honour, to Antigonos Doson in 222, after his victory at Sellasia, and to Philip V in 218.

The second century is obviously a period of uncertainty. Inscriptions and offerings which can be dated to this period are most infrequent. As relations between Rome and the Greeks deteriorated, conditions in the Aegean area became increasingly unsettled and, in general terms, the fortunes of the sanctuary reflect this. Epidauros had established early contact with Rome; Livy recorded[24] that in 292 BC Epidauros, at the request of Roman envoys, sent a sacred snake to Rome to establish the cult of Asklepios there. This does not seem to have conferred any great, or immediate, benefit on the sanctuary.

In the chaos caused by the disintegration of Roman authority the sanctuary suffered with the rest of Greece.[25] The Roman dictator Sulla confiscated its treasures (along with those of Olympia) to pay for his siege of Athens which had sided with Rome's enemy Mithridates of Pontus. Worse was to follow as Roman affairs relapsed into civil war. The Aegean was overrun by sea-borne plunderers who sacked the sanctuary, together with those at Hermione, Kalaureia and Isthmia itself. It is not possible to say how extensive the damage was; obviously movable treasures were more vulnerable than buildings, but it is not unreasonable to suppose that some physical damage was done, particularly to buildings constructed in unbaked mud brick. With the end of the Roman civil wars, and the institution of the principate of Augustus, the fortunes of Greece, and Epidauros, revived. There is a sequence of dedications to the imperial family; to the emperor's wife, Livia, his stepsons Drusus and Tiberius, to his grandson Lucius. The sequence extends into the first century AD; Tiberius as emperor, Drusilla the sister of Caligula, Claudius and his wives Agrippina and Messalina. The great families of Greece also took an interest in Epidauros: there is a base from a statue dedicated to Gaius Julius Eurykles. From the second century AD there is an interesting inscription recording the healing of a man from Mylasa in Caria, whose name, M. Julius Idrieus, recalls one of the Carian dynasts of the fourth century BC.

All this evidence points to the sanctuary continuing to function, even if at times in a modest way, but with renewed interest in the early years of the Roman Empire. A more significant redevelopment belongs to the second century AD. This is referred to by Pausanias,[26] who attributes contemporary buildings to 'the senator Antoninus': a bath of Asklepios, a building outside the sanctuary for the dying and women giving birth (who were by taboo excluded from the sanctuary) and the rebuilding of the Portico of Kotys, which had been ruined. This information is confirmed by the archaeological discoveries; there is extensive Roman construction in the sanctuary, including the repair or alteration in brick and mortared work of earlier structures. Tiles used in this are stamped with the name Antoninus. It is often assumed that this must be Antoninus Pius, the emperor, though the way Pausanias merely calls him a 'Roman Senator' is curious. The German scholar Hiller von Gaertringen suggested[27] that it was not the emperor at all, but another man, of Greek origin, who had adopted the same Roman name, and who had become a Roman senator, Sextus Iulius Maior Antoninus Pythorus of Nysa in Asia Minor. The repairs are extensive, and it would appear that the sanctuary was in some decay; but most of the work, as Pausanias states in the case of the portico of

Kotys, was carried out in buildings whose superstructure was originally of unbaked mud-brick, and where collapse was inevitable with the passage of time. The decay was more likely caused by perennial shortage of funds, rather than general neglect, and this Antoninus must have made good from his own personal fortunes.

As a religious centre, there is no reason to doubt the continued importance of the sanctuary throughout this period, and, in the same way, into the third century AD when once more political instability descended in the Mediterranean world. Like most of southern Greece, Epidauros was plundered and probably badly damaged by barbarian invaders, the Heruls. Subsequent to this a defensive wall, constructed from the rubble of destroyed buildings, was thrown round the inner part of the sanctuary. The cult continued, and priests of Asklepios were still making dedications when the Roman Empire officially recognized Christianity. The sanctuary then entered its ultimate phase.

There are obvious points of similarity between the myth, legends and achievements of the Asklepios cult and Christianity.[28] Both religions centre on a figure who was the son of a divinity by a mortal woman, who had miraculous powers of healing, including the power to raise the dead, who died, was buried in a tomb which became a place of cult, and who had himself divine status after death.

It is, of course, a comparison which was already made in antiquity; and which worried the Christian authors and apologists. For example, Justin: 'When the devil produces Asklepios as the raiser of the dead, and the healer of other diseases, do I not say in the same way that in this matter also he had imitated the prophecies about Christ?'[29]

The fact that Asklepios was often given the title of Saviour invoked direct competition with Christianity; this is made clear in the account given by Eusebius[30] of the destruction by Constantine of the temple of Asklepios at Aigai in Cilicia. Such destruction was most unusual, despite the conversion of the Empire to Christianity, pagan temples normally being left untouched (though it is probable that their landed property was confiscated). There may have been special reasons why this particular temple was selected, for the other temples of Asklepios were apparently unharmed, but the main reason seems to be its prominence, which drew attention to beliefs which to the righteous must have appeared blasphemous parodies of Christianity.

This is emphasized by the attempt, later in the century, of the Emperor Julian to restore the Empire to paganism. Julian now was reacting against the Christianity of the imperial family, to which he belonged, and of the Empire, and seeking to replace it with an organized paganism. In his writings he refers to Asklepios in terms which directly recall Christian belief about Christ himself:[31]

Since he [the Sun, Helios] fills the whole of our life with order, he begets
Asklepios in the world [kosmos]: but he has him with him even before the
beginning of the world.

Shall I now go on to tell you how Helios took thought for the health and
safety of all by begetting Asklepios to be the Saviour of the whole world?

This powerful support for the old cult is anticipated, a few years
before the accession of Julian, at Epidauros itself when, in AD 355
Mnaseas, the last known priest and *hierophant* of the Saviour,
dedicated an altar to Asklepios – not to any of the earlier forms of
Asklepios recorded at Epidauros, but to Asklepios of Aigai.[32]

At Aigai itself, Julian ordered the church which had been built from
the debris of the temple to be pulled down, and the temple rebuilt. He
died before the work had progressed; his revived paganism died with
him, and the church was restored. Julian's ideas concerning Asklepios
were refuted by the Christian apologists.

In this context we must put the final abandonment of the Epidaurian
sanctuary. The visitor to Epidauros cannot but notice the thoroughness
of the ruin which has afflicted the whole sanctuary, except for the
Theatre and a few solidly built Roman brick and concrete constructions. Superficially other sanctuaries were equally devastated. Olympia
is an example, but there clear evidence survived of gradual decay and
eventual collapse as the result of an earthquake. The great columns of
the Temple of Zeus still lie there as they fell, as mute witness to this
natural catastrophe. In contrast, there is little of the superstructure
surviving at Epidauros. The Theatre, mercifully, was covered by
landslip and vegetation, so that it has survived (though the stage
building, presumably not covered in this way, has been stripped
mercilessly). Of the other buildings, the fragmentary pieces are
collected in the Museum. Much, no doubt, was removed for building
stone, some to Ligourio, some perhaps further afield (though there are
not many places in easy reach). Some, probably, was destroyed in the
weathering processes to which certain of the building materials used –
particularly the stone from Corinth – are very susceptible. But neither
seems to explain completely such total destruction and it is not
impossible that, with the restoration of Christianity and the particularly close challenge presented by Julian's Asklepios, Constantine's
destruction of the sanctuary at Aigai – levelled to the ground – was
also inflicted on Epidauros. Certainly the description fits.

Even so, this was not the complete end. In the north-eastern part of
the sanctuary, close to the Propylon, are the remains of a substantial
Christian church, together with the forecourt. Though ruined, like the
rest of the sanctuary, there is a fair amount of its superstructure about
it. It is certainly the religious successor in possession of the site;
whether it was also a successor in other respects we know not.

PART II THE MONUMENTS

Building materials

The sanctuary was built essentially from various types of limestone. Much undoubtedly comes from local quarries, since transport adds considerably to the cost of the material, but in several important instances the building accounts require stone from further afield. Thus, for the Temple of Asklepios the stone for the foundations under the external colonnade is contracted for by Mnasikles, an Epidaurian; the presumption therefore is that the stone was local, and this is indeed confirmed by the actual remains. The columns, on the other hand, are contracted for by Lykios of Corinth. This Corinthian limestone was shipped from the harbour of Kenchreai to Epidauros, and then hauled up to the sanctuary. It is an attractive stone, weathering to a golden yellow in colour. It cuts easily and accurately – it is, obviously, a much easier stone to work than marble, and this in part explains the great rapidity with which it was possible to build this temple compared, for example, with the Parthenon. So long as the buildings were intact it was fairly durable, but when exposed to the weather it crumbles badly. This is particularly noticeable in the Temple of Asklepios where blocks which were not intended to be exposed have suffered for a century from the ravages of weather, and more recently from the hordes of visitors, and are reduced to a crumbled mass. Fortunately, this has now been fenced off, but elsewhere in the sanctuary there are still many exposed surfaces of this stone, and the considerate visitor should avoid treading on them. Significantly, this stone was not used for the floors and the entrance ramp. Kavvadias thought that fragments of a black limestone which he found inside the *cella* of the Temple came from its floor; but Roux has demonstrated that this is probably too fragile for flooring material, and suggests rather that it decorated a monumental base.

Later in the fourth century much more use was made of hard local limestone. A coarse-grained local stone was already used in the foundations of the Temple of Asklepios; and in various forms (where local origin is presumed, rather than certain) it seems also to have been used in later superstructures; in the Temple of Artemis, for example, and, in a particularly attractive, pink-toned form, in the walls of the great Banqueting Hall. A pink-toned limestone occurs also in the Theatre. At present a very similar stone is produced from a quarry behind the modern village of Ligourio. In the Banqueting Hall and several other buildings the hard stone is used only for the vulnerable footings and lower sections of wall, where durability was essential; the upper parts were made from unbaked mud brick, of which no trace remains (though when he excavated Kavvadias often reported that the soil he removed was formed from collapsed and washed-out mud brick). It is a cheap, effective and (again, if properly protected) durable building material.

Pentelic marble was used sparingly; costs of quarrying and transport from the quarries to Piraeus must have been higher than the corresponding costs of extracting Corinthian stone and transporting it to Kenchreai. Nevertheless a fair quantity of it was used for the Thymele. On the exterior it was used for the elaborately carved *sima* (gutter) and decorative course of the wall, and the ceiling, but inside the Corinthian columns and entablature were entirely of Pentelic marble, and it was combined with the black stone for the elaborate and spectacularly effective floor. The black stone was also used as a contrasting colour in the wall. The most noticeable use of marble in this building was undoubtedly for the tiles and the crowning decoration of the roof.

In the Temple of Asklepios, on the other hand, the tiles were of terracotta; and this was normal in the other buildings. The colour contrast to the marble tiles of the Thymele must have been very obvious. Terracotta was also used in less important buildings for decorative elements, such as the gutters, which were otherwise made in marble or stone.

Timber, of course, is another essential material, for roof beams and doors, which inevitably has perished totally. It should also be noticed that wood might have been used instead of stone columns for vertical supports in places where the stonework (*stylobate*) seems too narrow to have supported columns of normal dimensions (for example, in the inner court of the Portico of Kotys); elsewhere small stone plinths may well have supported wooden posts. The building inscriptions give fullest evidence for the types of timber used; archaeologically the only evidence for timber consists of the cuttings in blocks of stone to receive the beams. For the Temple of Asklepios Lykios of Corinth was paid 4,390 drachmas for pine wood (which he had probably acquired by trade). Tychamenes of Crete is paid an uncertain amount for cypress wood. These would be construction timbers. Sotairos supplied elm wood, lotus-tree wood and box wood for the door. Later he received the contract for ivory used in the decoration of the door; not surprisingly, this cost 3,150 drachmas, as opposed to 840 for the timber, part of which was, in any case, used for a workshop (**20**).

When it is preserved the stonework of the fourth century and Hellenistic age can easily be recognized by its characteristic features –

large blocks of stone, precisely fitted together, and joined, where the surface was to be covered, with iron clamps set in lead; these rarely survive, but the cuttings for them are noticeable. The earliest (in the well by the Propylon, which may antedate the development of the cult of Asklepios) are ⌐‿⌐ in shape; then ⊢——⊣, as in the Temple of Asklepios (both are *plan* shapes); and finally in the buildings of the later fourth century and after ⌐———⌐ in shape (as seen in profile). Surfaces of steps, floors and walls were polished smooth; the entablatures received the usual painted or carved decoration. The stone footings to mud-brick walls are often given a rusticated surface to give an impression of ruggedness in contrast to the smooth stucco coating which would have been applied over the mud brick. Other decorative treatment of stone surfaces is less common. Steps were often undercut (and this would be more noticeable if more were preserved). The 'workshop' building has a wall whose blocks are decorated with rows of short vertical chisel marks. Such a pattern usually indicates a Hellenistic date, but where it recurs, in the courtyard building between the Temple of Artemis and the Banqueting Hall, the simultaneous employment of rubble, and the fact that some of the decorated blocks are put sideways, shows that we here have an example of re-used material, and thus the building, as it now is, is Roman in date.

Original Roman work is easily recognized. Unlike the Greek it uses lime mortar to bind together walls of baked brick, or small rubble, or combinations of both. This invariably looks rough compared with polished Greek stonework. It should be remembered that these walls were once coated, either with stucco or thin veneers of polished stone. There are surviving traces of this in the North-East Baths. The earlier work (belonging to the second century AD), that carried out by 'Antoninus', the Roman Senator, uses nice regularly coursed brickwork; but as rougher work is also attested (by tiles bearing Antoninus' name) from this period, a casual inspection is not enough to distinguish earlier from later Roman work. Much more confusing is the re-use made by the Romans of earlier material. Sometimes this is a matter of repair; Greek footings, for example, may survive from the original building where the superstructure is replaced by Roman mortared construction (replacing, perhaps, unbaked brickwork of the Greek period). Here apparently Roman buildings in reality go back to the Greek period. In other instances stones from Greek walls are removed bodily and re-used perhaps in repairs, perhaps in new buildings. There is a good example in the North-East Baths, where a good run of Greek limestone blocks is visible, but set over a Roman mortared rubble footing, and probably represents a repair of the Epidoteion to which they belong. Here apparently Greek work belongs in fact to Roman

construction, and, although much is reconstruction, a lot occurs in
buildings which are essentially new developments. Different types of
Roman mortar construction can be seen clearly. The Odeion constructed in the courtyard of the Banqueting Hall, where it does not
incorporate original Greek stonework, employs rubble work with
good-quality pinkish mortar, in bands separated by brick string-
courses, each with from one to four layers of brick. The regularity of
the work is noticeable. Similar construction, with string-courses of
brick with up to five or even six layers of brick, occurs in the Roman
North-East Baths. This clearly is the style employed in the thorough-
going and methodical reconstruction carried out during the second
century AD.

On the other hand, the small courtyard building next to the
Banqueting Hall has walls that incorporate a footing of re-used Greek
masonry, but with the mortared work entirely of rubble. The string-
courses in this case consist of broken fragments of brick and tile,
obviously re-used from earlier structures. The mortar is more white
than pink. The total effect is much cruder, and such construction
probably belongs to a later period than the first (Kavvadias thought in
terms of a late third century AD reconstruction, after the Herul
destruction). The courtyard house to the east uses rubble with very
little brick, and white mortar – this seems an even cruder variant of the
late technique.

Part of the North-East Baths, the apse of the main hall with its
curved surface, is entirely in brick – again, an indication of the
good-quality construction in the Roman work of this period. There is
another variant of careful technique in the substantial, well-preserved
but much overgrown building in the north-west part of the sanctuary.
The tower has all-brick exterior surfaces, including the part facing
towards the courtyard, while the inner surfaces at the corners only are
also all brick; the remainder of this structure is of rubble, with odd
pieces of brick. To the west, the main building is of rubble with brick
string-courses, as in the Odeion and the bath building.

Finally, there are the late-Roman fortifications which enclosed the
centre of the sanctuary. Here the material is all re-used (or random
rubble) from any previous period in building. It can be distinguished
by the totally random way in which the earlier material is re-employed,
and by its general layout: two long straight lines (the inner and outer
faces) with rubble or other fill between.

Too little survives of the superstructures to say much about what can
actually be observed in terms of construction method. Most of the
Greek buildings were of the normal trabeated type; that is, columns
and walls supported the timber beams and rafters of the roof. Some of

the blocks for the upper parts of the walls, and the entablature blocks, in the Museum have the cuttings into which the beams were slotted. The position of the outer ceiling of the peripteral Temple of Asklepios was only a little above the top of the architrave, in the fourth-century manner. In the Thymele (Tholos), this is of course replaced by a stone ceiling (the interior woodwork cannot be reconstructed, and the domed form suggested by Kavvadias and illustrated in a picture in the Museum is most implausible). Hellenistic arches and vaults occur; the obvious example (though at the moment difficult of access) is the vaulted passageway which leads from the Gymnasium under the bank of seating into the Stadium. The large rectangular cistern to the north-west of the Abaton has a series of buttresses projecting from the side walls. Each side was probably once linked with an arch, the top being continuous and supporting an overall floor. Nothing of these arches now survives, but there is another, better preserved cistern, of essentially the same type, just below the Sanctuary of Apollo Maleatas, where the beginning of the arches is clearly visible.

With Roman mortared construction, roofing, of course, becomes more ambitious. There are several vaults of both early and late periods, in the main sanctuary and in the Roman construction in the Maleatas sanctuary. In one of the rooms of the North-East Baths, to the south of the central hall, are just visible the remains of a cross-vaulted ceiling.

Propylon

From a distance, as one approaches along the road from Ligourio, the sanctuary is dominated by the Theatre (figure 3), the regular symmetry of its seats standing out clearly against the hillside. It is not surprising that the modern road leads towards this, ending at a car park on the southern side of the sanctuary. From here, if he looks towards the sanctuary, the visitor will notice a large and confused expanse of ruined buildings, mostly reduced to their footings. Beyond the car park the road becomes a pedestrian walk through pleasant gardens shaded by trees; here is the present entrance, by the Museum, and with the Theatre only a short distance beyond. It is tempting to go to it first, but this is a mistake. The Theatre is, of course, the best preserved and the most impressive of the remains at Epidauros. The ancient approach to the sanctuary was from the opposite, northern side. The sanctuary is more intelligible if it is allowed to reveal itself in its original sequence; so the visitor should, for the moment, ignore the Theatre, go past the entrance to the Museum and make his way

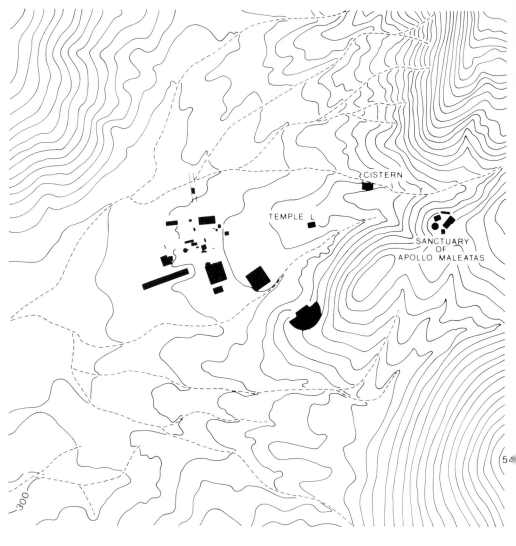

CISTERN

TEMPLE L

SANCTUARY
OF
APOLLO MALEATAS

54

Contours at 10m intervals

0   200   400   600   800   1000
                                                    M

3 The two sanctuaries: general layout

through the buildings clustered round the Temple of Asklepios, to the
Propylon (figures 4 and 5).

Here, at the northern boundary of the sanctuary (and at its lowest
point), the ancient road from Epidauros crossed a small stream (now
just outside the modern perimeter fence). The Propylon (**1**) lies

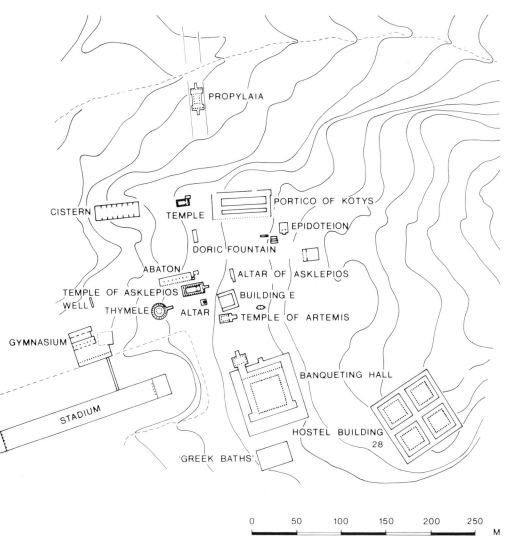

PROPYLAIA

CISTERN

TEMPLE

PORTICO OF KOTYS

EPIDOTEION

DORIC FOUNTAIN

ABATON

ALTAR OF ASKLEPIOS

TEMPLE OF ASKLEPIOS

WELL

THYMELE

ALTAR

BUILDING E

TEMPLE OF ARTEMIS

GYMNASIUM

BANQUETING HALL

STADIUM

HOSTEL BUILDING
28

'GREEK BATHS'

0   50   100   150   200   250

M

4 Sanctuary of Asklepios: the Greek buildings (except the Theatre)

immediately to the south of this. It was very much a formal decorative
entrance. The sanctuary certainly had a clearly defined boundary,
separating the sacred area from the profane world beyond. Pausanias
tells us that the boundary was marked and that meat from the
sacrificial victims had to be consumed within the *peribolos*, the
boundary of the sanctuary. There are now no traces visible of this
boundary – and it seems that it was never a physical barrier, but rather
a line of posts or marker stones.

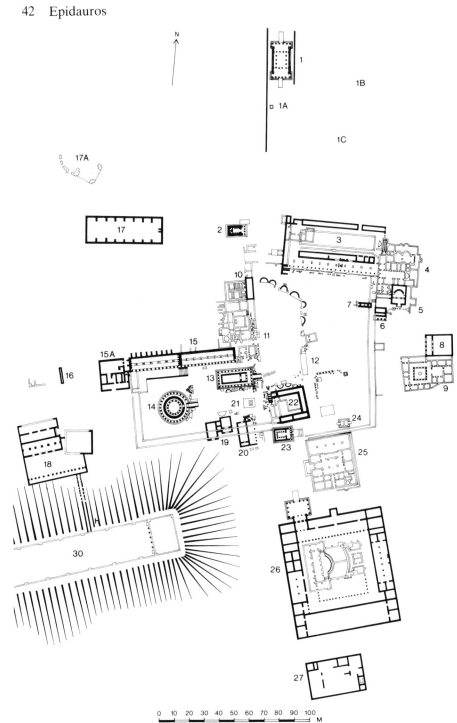

5 Sanctuary of Asklepios: the main area

6 Reconstruction of the sanctuary

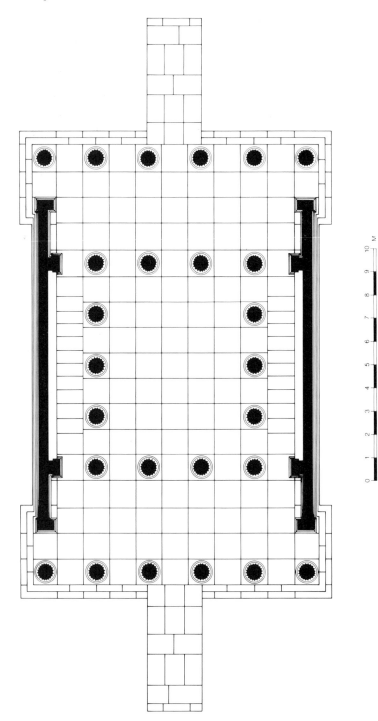

7 The Propylon (*after G. Roux*)

2 The Propylon: the outer ramped approach

In any case the Epidaurian Propylon (unlike the Propylaia of the Athenian Acropolis) had no doors which could be closed, and there were clear passages to either side.

It consists of a raised base, 14.39 × 20.3 m (plate 2 and figure 7). There are steps at either end but the normal approach is by central ramps (such ramps are a noticeable feature of all the principal buildings at Epidauros). The superstructure has fallen, but there were once six Doric columns above the steps, with walls along the sides; these walls terminated behind the outermost columns of the façades, and the steps turned back to meet them. Normally in gateway buildings the side walls would be joined by a cross wall, pierced only by a doorway (or, as in Athenian propylaia, a set of doorways) which could be closed. There is no cross wall of this type in the Epidaurian Propylon. Instead, there is a square of 4×4 m Corinthian columns, the outer and inner rows being aligned with pilasters engaged against the side walls. The roof was of the normal ridge type, with a pediment at either end.

This building makes a very emphatic architectural flourish at the entrance to the sanctuary. It may have served a more specific purpose. There are other gateways which cannot have been complete barriers to sanctuaries; the South Propylon to the sanctuary of Zeus at Labraunda in Caria, for example, also has clear passageways to either side, though the building itself is of the normal type, with a cross-wall and a door

3 The early well by the Propylon

which could be closed. The interior of the Epidauros Propylon resembles that of the temples, with their decorative inner colonnades. The architectural flourish, then, is more than mere external appearance, for which only the façades are essential. The interior is, in effect, a room, and that should mean a place in which to pause in the ceremonial approach for prayer or supplication on entering the sanctuary. The ramps would have made it possible for processions to enter with dignity. The Propylon makes less sense as a building through which casual visitors entered the sanctuary, though this is not to say that they were necessarily sent round the side, or through some other 'tradesmen's entrance', as it were. It is the formal aspect which gives rise to the design, which announces that here whoever passes through, under whatever auspices, leaves the profane world and enters the sanctified area.

From the Propylon to the next group of buildings belonging to the original sanctuary is still an appreciable distance – some 75 m. The processional way is lined on either side with a wall. On the right-hand side is a well (**1A**) whose blocks are fixed together with ⌐‿⌐ clamps, an indication of an early date, in the sixth or, at latest, early fifth century BC (plate 3). Thus it belongs to the time when the sanctuary was undeveloped; though its position suggests that even at this date the boundaries of the sacred area were defined at the limits implied by the position of the Propylon.

The date of the Propylon can be established only by the forms of its architecture; Roux suggests, on these grounds, the early part of the third century BC and it is reasonable to accept this. Miss Burford argues for an earlier date, for the less cogent reason that an impressive Propylon is an early requirement for the developed sanctuary,[33] but, if the area had existed for so long without such embellishment at its boundaries, perhaps such a building was less pressing. Even if a pause in the movement of the procession is likely as an explanation of its architectural form, ritually this was less important than the architectural requirements satisfied by the proved early structures of the development, the Temple, the Thymele and (even if not proven) the Abaton.

Though there are no other buildings of the original sanctuary in the vicinity of the Propylon, the visitor will find the remains of later structures. To the east is an early Christian church (**1B**), rarely visited and often overgrown.[34] It is of the usual basilical type, with nave and aisles. In front of its west end is a courtyard (atrium) and at the northern side a second small church or chapel. Though ruined, the remains of these buildings are quite substantial, and they form a poignant last witness to the continued religious importance of the area, even when converted to the new faith.

Further to the south, but still on the eastern side of the road from the Propylon, is a late house (**1C**), in badly ruined state.

Portico of Kotys and related buildings

The road leads straight from the Propylon to the heart of the sanctuary, which it reaches after climbing a sharply rising bank. After this bank, the ancient road passes between the front of a small temple to the west and, to the east, the end of a portico which faced southwards onto the main, central part of the sanctuary.

The temple (**2**) is small and in a very poor state. Only foundations can be made out (and with difficulty), measuring 13.56 × 7.42 m. They are made of a pinkish poros (soft limestone) which is crumbling badly. They had already partly disappeared at the time of the original excavations; the plan then made cannot now be verified. The reconstruction is even more uncertain; Roux[35] gives as alternatives a prostyle façade, of four columns, or two in antis, preferring the former because of a marked predilection at Epidauros for prostyle temples. There is no evidence for the order. At the back of the *cella* is the base for the cult statue – but what cult is unknown. It *could* be a temple of Themis. Despite its small size, a foundation runs round the inside of the *cella* wall for an internal colonnade. This was presumably Corinthian, and fragments of a Corinthian capital in poros have been identified with this. There are no structural reasons for such a colonnade; it must be purely decorative, following a fashion which was established with the Temple of Asklepios itself.

There is no trace of the altar. A huge rectangular foundation is placed along the front part of the north side, but this is for the base of a statue; from the shape of the base, it was probably equestrian.

The building (3) to the east of the road is substantial, and by Epidaurian standards quite well preserved, though partly confused by later structures (plate 4). It measures approximately 63 × 31.5 m. To accommodate it the ground, which rises gently to the east, had to be levelled by cutting away at the east and terracing at the west. There is a long, rather narrow internal courtyard, surrounded by a peristyle. No columns survive from this, and as their foundation is very narrow they were probably wooden. Behind the peristyle on the north, south and west was a row of rooms (the eastern end is totally obscured by the subsequent construction of the Roman baths). Outside the south and west walls was a Doric stoa facing south onto the central area of the sanctuary, and west onto the road, with stone columns about 4.70 m high and, probably, a wooden entablature. There was an inner Ionic colonnade. Visually this building was important in that it provided a substantial and interesting border to the northern side of the central area. From the details of the Doric capitals, the building appears to date to the early Hellenistic period, perhaps the first half of the third century BC. If so, like the Propylon, it indicates that at this period buildings were planned whose function, in part at least, was to embellish the sanctuary. The walls are of mud-brick on a stone footing. Roux[36] believes that it is the Portico of Kotys, mentioned by Pausanias as being in a state of ruin, the mud-brick walls having dissolved because of the collapse of the roof. The building believed by Kavvadias to be the Portico of Kotys (and still labelled as such on the monument itself and in the popular guide books), which is on the other side of the central area (25) is much later in date in its surviving form, and is certainly Roman. It comprises rooms arranged round a courtyard and thus hardly qualifies as a portico. The Doric colonnade of building (3) makes it much more likely that this was the Portico of Kotys.

The buildings on the east side of the central area form an interesting group. The majority of the visible walls (which are quite substantial) belong obviously to the Roman North-East Baths (4), being of mortared baked bricks and rubble. There are several earlier structures.

First, on the eastern side of the Roman Baths, and partly embedded

4 The Portico of Kotys: stylobate and drainage channel

in them, is a nearly square structure (**5**) 11.75 × 12.70 m, divided into two by a poros foundation, and with a square projection on its south side. The walls are largely mortared and contemporary (or a little earlier) with the Roman Baths, but these are a late repair, re-using earlier material, and are built on a base with upright slabs (orthostats) and crowning course of good Greek workmanship (perhaps the original superstructure was mud-brick). The southern half had a floor of pebbles set in cement, and the presence of a terracotta drain suggests that it was unroofed – it may have contained an altar. The northern half, behind the substantial poros dividing-foundation, is largely occupied by a curved base in limestone. The foundation may have supported a low wall or podium, with a central opening and two columns. The curved base must have been made for a statue group; fragments of the torso from a marble statue of Asklepios, over life-size, found in the vicinity, belong to this. In his description Pausanias mentions, in a passage which, perhaps, refers to this part of the sanctuary, the 'hieron' of the Epidotes, the Helpful Gods, with a Temple of Health, Apollo and Egyptian Asklepios. There seems little doubt that this structure should be identified with the hieron. An inscription, probably of the fourth century BC, refers to the Epidoteion and its original construction. It mentions statues and a hearth, so there may have been this hearth rather than an altar in the southern part. What can now be seen is presumably a reconstruction, employing the original material, of this fourth-century construction. The projection on the south side is the entrance.

In front of the Epidoteion, and slightly to the west, are the remains of a Fountain House (**6**) which faced south. It had a façade of four columns (Roux suggests Doric, but there is no evidence for this, and Ionic is just as likely). Behind the façade was a square structure (c. 4.60 × 4.60 m) divided into two. The northern part, completely enclosed, was a storage chamber; in front of this, a draw-basin. The water supply was provided by a covered conduit which runs in from the east. Immediately against the eastern wall is a small basin which serves as a diversion and settling-tank. The water is led into a channel behind the back wall of the draw-basin, into which it once fed water through three lion-head spouts. After the westernmost spout the channel continues to supply the storage chamber. There was no connection between the storage chamber and the draw-basin, which was supplied only with freshly flowing water from the conduit.

The storage chamber supplied a second fountain (**7**) to the west. A long narrow structure, 11.50 × 3.45 m, it is another Roman replacement for a similar earlier building. The entrance is from the west, by a narrow doorway which leads into a small courtyard. At the end of this

5 The North-East Baths, showing Roman brick and rubble construction, and re-used Greek squared stone

a corridor leads to a basin. The door to the corridor employs a moulded cornice of undoubted Hellenistic date, over an 'arch' (in fact cut in a single block of stone). The orthostats of the walls also appear Hellenistic in date. This fountain probably had a cult-function.

Roux dates the original construction of this complex of waterworks to around the middle of the third century, but these dates are uncertain; they could (like the Portico of Kotys) be fifty years earlier. There are indications (a pebble floor outside the 'sacred' fountain) of earlier construction. The continued existence of these fountains in the Roman period, and the construction of the substantial Roman Bath building in the same area, indicates that there was a good source of water in the immediate vicinity – good, but not overwhelmingly plentiful, since the fountains include arrangements for storage. It is this water source, and the existence of other sources in the area, which account for the original development of the lower sanctuary.

To the south-east of the Epidoteion is a rectangular structure (**8**), 18.45 × 13.95 m. Four Doric columns between *antae*, which terminate short returns along the façade from the side walls, open into an ante-chamber whose rear wall is 4.30 m behind the colonnade. Three doors in this wall lead to a courtyard. This building seems to belong to the fourth century. Its identification and function are uncertain. A courtyard building (**9**), the 'Roman House', was constructed alongside it in the late-Roman period.

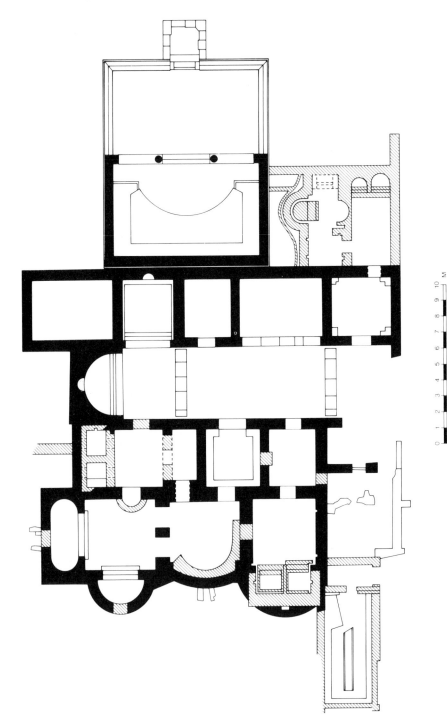

8 The North-East Baths (*after R. Ginouvès*)

A final element in the archaeological complexity of this region is the late defensive wall, which was put round the remains of the central buildings, probably in the late fourth century AD. A clear section of this runs south from the Roman Baths, turning to the west by building (9). It must be distinguished from earlier structures which were part of the sanctuary.

The most important Roman building in this whole area is the North-East Baths (4) which belong essentially to the main Roman phase of reconstruction in the second century AD although pieces of older Greek buildings are incorporated into their fabric. The good quality mortared work (plate 5), stone with brick string-courses, is of the second century. Their arrangement is comparable with that of other bath buildings of the period in this part of Greece (figure 8). The entrance appears to have been on the west side, now badly damaged, near the Portico of Kotys. A stylobate once supported monolithic columns which now lie fallen in the main hall to which they once gave access. With its vestibule, the hall runs the full depth of the building, some 19.5 m from west to east; it is 8.8 m wide. There was another colonnade at its eastern end beyond which was a semicircular plunge bath. This central hall corresponds to the great hall of the imperial bath buildings at Rome, and is best identified as the cold room, the *frigidarium*. There are extensions of this room to the south, including a cold pool. On the other side is a series of warm rooms. The two to the west are still directly accessible from the main hall, but the easternmost, the largest of them, with a heated plunge bath at its western end had its original entrance doorway blocked off. From these rooms bathers proceeded to the suite on the northern side of the building, the main heated rooms. Again doorways have been subsequently blocked and new openings made. A well-preserved section of hypocaust, the underfloor heating, is visible in the western room.

The alterations are in much cruder rubble work, and probably much later in date. They include the provision of a small additional bathing suite in the south-west corner, in front of the Epidoteion, perhaps serving as a separate bath for women. Otherwise the principal effect of the alterations, as René Ginouvès points out in his study of them,[37] is to divide several of the rooms into small individual baths. He suggests this is the result not so much of changes in attitude in the Late Empire, which turned from the use of large communal baths because of a new sense of shame and modesty in the face of nakedness, but rather to allow for separate washing by the individual who could then adjust the temperature to his own requirements. He dates the alterations to the late fourth or fifth century, though probably they belong to the period before the construction of the defensive wall.

The bath building in its present state appears, at a first glance, to be a rather shoddy structure, in contrast to the fine stonework employed in the earlier Greek buildings. This is misleading. There are still traces of decoration applied within the mortared walls which must have transformed their appearance. The fine stone columns of the main hall are examples of this decorative work, for they hardly served a mere structural purpose. There are fragments of the finish applied to the walls, and some of the rooms still preserve their mosaic floors, though these, exposed to the elements by the excavations and now totally unprotected, are fast decaying.

The west side of the central area, beyond the small temple (2), is marked by a cluster of buildings lining the road. Most of these are late, but they include, about 20 m south of the temple, a third-century-BC structure (10). This is partly encumbered with later walls, but under these are foundations of limestone of the type used in the main period of development to support mud-brick walls; the Roman structures replace these. The foundations mark the west side of an enclosure, 13.60 × 5.50 m. The south side was defined by a different wall, of the poros foundations used in the main period for more substantial walls, but again these have been replaced by later structure. The whole of this area is in a confused state, only partly excavated and needing re-excavation to make a thorough study feasible. The other sides of the enclosure are defined by a base on a poros foundation, forming three narrow steps. There is a ramp at the eastern end, and this must have been the only entrance, for the steps are too narrow to be of practical use. There is no good evidence for the superstructure but Roux[38] points out that a stepped base implies more than a plain wall; he restores a wall decorated with a series of engaged pilasters, as at building (24) ('Peribolos Y') to the east of the Temple of Artemis.

These buildings occupy the northern section on the west side of the road. The southern part is marked by the end of a fifth-century-BC building (11) and then the façade of the Temple of Asklepios.

In the centre of this central area, arranged to form a curving line reaching from the Portico of Kotys (3) to the Altar of Asklepios (12), is a line of *exedrai*, stone seats, mostly semicircular in plan. They face towards the Temple (13) or at least to the general area in front of it. Beyond the Altar there is another line of them, placed close to the wall of Building E (22).

The Temple of Asklepios

The Altar of Asklepios, of which only the foundations remain, was long and narrow, in contrast to that of Apollo (21) which was square.

Similar long altars are common in this part of Greece; they occur, for example, at Isthmia, and at the sanctuary of Hera at Perachora. They are not restricted to any one deity, and are best explained as a regional type. Usually they are decorated with a triglyph frieze; an alternative (Ionic) has plain sides with a moulded decoration at top and bottom. It is not certain which type the Altar of Asklepios employed. The Altar of Apollo Maleatas, in the upper sanctuary, was Ionic. There is in the Museum a dedicatory model of a triglyph altar which may have been intended as a replica of Asklepios' own altar.

The Altar is placed slightly to one side of the central axis of the Temple; it is displaced by the pre-existing and presumably significant Building E (**22**). There are the remains of a paved path connecting the ramp at the front of the Temple with the Altar.

If all these structures help define the central area, its importance nevertheless derives from the principal buildings to which it gives access: the Temple and Altar of Asklepios, the Abaton, the Thymele. All these belong to the fourth-century development; but the area was already established as the most important, most sacred part of the sanctuary, and in fact the fourth-century buildings were somewhat constricted by the way the land slopes down to the north and east (though this does not completely explain the relatively small size of the Temple, which could have been built on a grander scale; availability of funds was probably the major factor here). The other constricting factor was the presence to the south of the original square altar (**21**) whose foundations are clearly visible. It is unlikely that this was demolished at the fourth-century development, and since Asklepios then had his own altar the probability must be that this was, and remained, Apollo's.

The construction of a full Temple to Asklepios (**13**) was an indication of the status the sanctuary had achieved. Previously the cult had functioned without a building on this scale; a temple is not an essential and inevitable part of the ritual. Even at Olympia a temple to Zeus was not built until the fifth century BC. Athens in the fifth century had built splendid temples of marble, not only to Athena on the Acropolis but at other sanctuaries, to Hephaistos, to Poseidon, to Ares, to Nemesis; and though some of these replaced earlier buildings, others were essentially new developments. Closer to Epidauros there was a new temple to Hera at the Argive Heraion. Other cities in the region already had peripteral temples: Aigina, Kalaureia, Hermione. There may have been peripteral temples already in Epidauros town and, even if there were not, given the attitude of the fourth century to the proper development of major sanctuaries, Asklepios clearly had to receive a suitable home.

6 The Temple of Asklepios

His Temple, then, was built in the Doric order, the normal style of the mainland (figures 9 and 10). The architect, as we learn from the building inscriptions, was Theodotos. It stood on a conventional platform of three steps of poros stone from Corinth over foundations of local stone. There is a ramp at the east end. Only the bottom step is at all well preserved (plate 6), but even this is complete only at the east end. Its vertical face is decorated by an undercut band along its lower edge. Of the upper steps only two middle-step blocks remain, with traces of the top step which was dowelled to them. The middle step also had the decorative band, and so, presumably, did the top step (other fourth-century Doric buildings, at Delphi for example, have a double band). The Corinthian stone has weathered badly in recent years, so that the whole platform has had to be fenced off. At its top the platform measured 23.28 × 12.03 m, its length being thus slightly under twice its width, dimensions comparable with those of the late sixth- early fifth-century Saronic Gulf group of temples, and shorter in proportion to the width than the fifth-century Athenian temples. There were six columns at each end, eleven along the flanks. The height of the columns cannot be measured from surviving blocks, but has been calculated, from the average height of the preserved drums, to have been about 5.7 m (ten drums of 0.54 plus the capital 0.304), or about 6.2 times the lower diameter, proportions which are suited to buildings of the fourth century BC. Corinthian poros is again the material used.

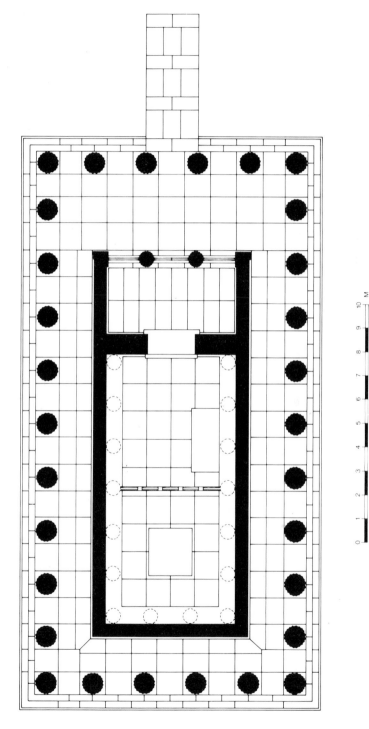

9 The Temple of Asklepios: plan (*after G. Roux*)

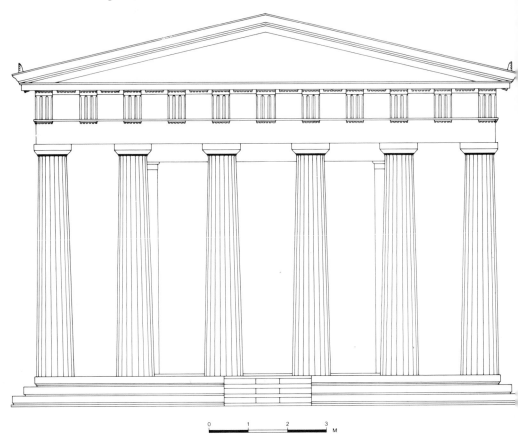

10 The Temple of Asklepios: façade restored

The metopes were not given carved decoration, but traces of red paint
have suggested the possibility of painted decoration. Enough of the
frieze survives for the measurement from centre to centre of the
triglyphs to be calculated; it is, to within 4 mm, identical to the spacing
of each step block of the platform. Since alternate triglyphs are centred
on the axis of the columns, and the columns themselves at their base
are centred on the upper step blocks, this implies that the columns
stood absolutely upright, without any of the complex inclination which
is found in Athenian architecture of the fifth century. Thus the Temple
is itself less sophisticated in design and, being easier to construct,
cheaper.

Marble was used sparingly for decorative elements. The continuous
gutter was of marble, with carved decoration, a flowing sequence of
acanthus scrolls punctuated by lion-head water spouts. The tiles, on

the other hand, were of terracotta. Even though the architecture is otherwise austere, with simplification apparent in the design, the pediments were fully decorated with marble sculpture. That at the east end represents the capture and destruction of Troy by the Greeks; the sculptor, who came from Athens, was Hektoridas. The western pediment contained a battle of Greeks and Amazons. The sculptor was again an Athenian, whose name began with the letters Theo-; he may be the architect. Both subjects are commonplace and though other examples may have an allegorical significance, symbolizing the struggle between the Greeks and the Persian barbarians, this does not seem relevant either to Epidauros or the cult of Asklepios. Over the pediments, at the lower angles and the peak, were decorative statues, *acroteria*. Those at the east end were females on horseback, perhaps personifying 'breezes', and were carved by Timotheos, another Athenian, and an important sculptor who was later involved in the decoration of the Mausoleum at Halikarnassos; the two lower figures survive, and are in the National Museum at Athens. The central *acroterion* included a representation of Epione. Those at the west end were by Theo-, and represented horsemen.

The inner part of the temple, whose substructures clearly reveal the plan, comprises a porch whose façade is aligned, as in several Athenian temples, with the third column of the flanks, leading to the *cella*. It differs from earlier temples by not having a false porch at the west end. The substructure of the *cella* has a single row of blocks supporting the porch wall and the doorway, and a wider foundation along the sides and at the end, the outer part supporting the footing of the wall, level with the top step of the platform. The wall was built on double upright slabs (orthostats) at the base, the outer having a moulding along its bottom edge, and with, perhaps, thirteen courses of regular ashlar blocks.

The total dimensions of the *cella* building are 6.81 × 16.45 m; the porch occupies 3.50 m of this length. No traces of the porch columns survive, but they were presumably in the same Doric order as the exterior; the epigraphic evidence speaks of carved decoration which would thus be the metopes (this is usual in Peloponnesian temples, Zeus at Olympia, the Argive Heraion, where only the inner, porch metopes were carved). Inside the *cella*, marks on surviving wall blocks demonstrate that there was an inner decoration, presumably columns, but again no trace of these has survived. The evidence of other buildings in the sanctuary suggests that they were in the Corinthian order, an early example of its employment in temple architecture.

Still visible at the Temple are the remains of the paving, long supporting blocks of stone laid flat on poros slabs, and which once carried the slabs of the floor. The foundations were not always adequate, and in places they have subsided. Ten of the supporting blocks survive at the east end. In the porch, two lines of foundations for the floor extend across the width. These supported two lines of slabs. In the *cella* only the base slabs remain, and it is not possible to decide whether the paving was of limestone slabs or a decorative floor in black and white, as in the Thymele; but the Temple of Artemis (**23**) had a slab floor, and this is more normal. One peculiarity of the floor is certain. The base slabs were omitted for a section against the south wall, giving a hollow 1.18 m wide and 2.70 m long, with a bottom about 0.50 m below the level of the now missing floor. It may have had a lid, and if so was probably a place for keeping a 'treasure', a special collection of sacred objects.

At the back of the *cella*, against the wall, was a wide base in poros, decorated with a veneer covering of thin black stone. This supported the cult statue, which has, of course, totally disappeared, but was described by Pausanias. The work of Thrasymedes, it was made, like Pheidias' Athena and Zeus, in gold and ivory over a wooden frame. Asklepios was represented seated on a throne, sceptre in hand and with a dog at his feet. As we have seen separate accounts were kept for the construction of this statue.

It is very difficult to visualize the original building from these fragmentary remains; even the elements put together in the Museum are not much help. Compared with, say, the Athenian temples, it was a modest enough structure. The material used in its construction was not the most expensive, in detail its design was simplified, factors which undoubtedly contributed to its relative cheapness and surprising rapidity of construction. Nevertheless it was in scale with the rest of the sanctuary. It had decent sculptural decoration, and the interior of the *cella*, at least, was made splendid and impressive by the Corinthian columns, an added luxury without any real structural function.

The Thymele

The circular Thymele, or Tholos (**14**) is situated behind and a little to the south of the Temple. Only the rings of its foundations are still in position (plate 7), though there is a considerable number of fragments of its superstructure, partly reconstructed with plaster additions, on display in the Museum. It is a substantial building, with a diameter of about 20 m (best measured at frieze level, 19.773 m). It is wider than the Temple (at 12.03 m), its columns were taller, and thus it was more imposing. It was lavishly decorated, and this fact, as well as its size,

7 The Thymele

marks it out as an important element in the sanctuary, more expensively and much more slowly built than the Temple.

The foundations consist of six concentric rings, made from tufa (figures 11 and 12). The three external rings, which once supported the outer colonnade, the *cella* wall and the inner colonnade, are naturally much more massive than the inner rings, which supported nothing of the main structure. There is no doubt that despite suggestions to the contrary, all six rings belong to one-and-the-same building phase. The inner rings are pierced by doors; although these now appear adjacent to each other, one can see slots in which barriers were once fixed from one ring to the next (plate 8), making it necessary to walk round the whole of one ring before coming to the doorway into the next. Thus the inner rings formed a simple maze. The innermost ring appears to surround a pit, but at the very centre there was once a pillar on which were fitted wooden steps whose other ends were supported by the ring wall (traces of this attachment are still visible). It is thus certain that it was intended that there should be access at the centre of the building through a hole in the floor (which may have had some form of trap door or cover over it) into the central substructures, and that within these substructures it was possible to move from ring to ring in a formal, indirect progression. It is also worth noting that little light would be admitted to the central ring, none at all to the next two. The outer rings were inaccessible.

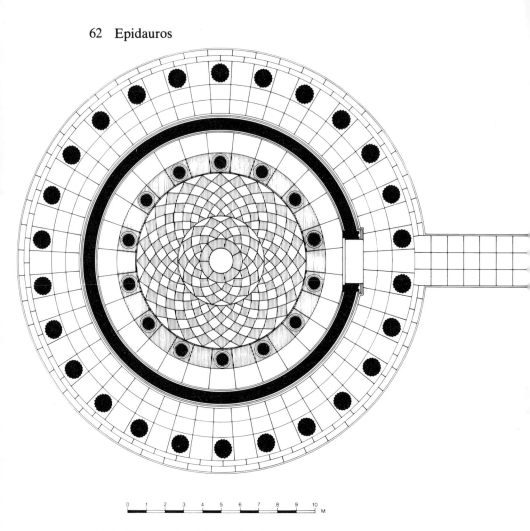

11 The Thymele: plan (*after G. Roux*)

On these foundations was erected a most spectacular superstructure. It was approached by the usual ramp from the east; otherwise the base had three steps. Very little of this survives, but enough to show that the steps increased in height from bottom to top: bottom step 0.275 m, middle step 0.285 m, top step 0.301 m. We do not know if they were plain or with decorative undercuttings, as in the Temple, but given the fourth-century tendency to decorate the steps of Doric buildings, and the lavish decoration in other respects of the Thymele, it is likely that this was done here also. On the top step was a ring of 26 Doric columns of poros. Of the 286 drums from which the columns were constructed, only 14 remain (and two of these are extremely fragmen-

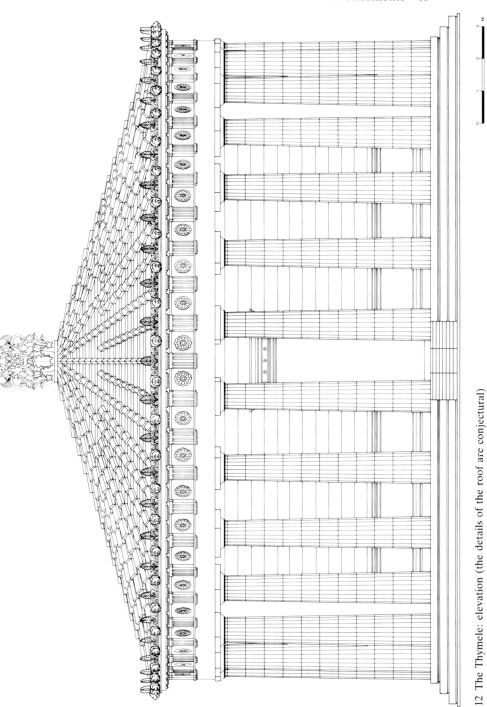

12 The Thymele: elevation (the details of the roof are conjectural)

8 Foundations of the Thymele, showing blocking partition

tary). Nevertheless they are sufficient to permit a reasonable reconstruction of the columns, with a height of 6.5 m, plus a capital 0.38 m
high. The total height, 6.88 m, is almost seven times the base diameter
of 0.992 m, more slender than the columns of the Temple (but in
circular buildings this is necessary to offset the proportionately greater
width, and need not in itself indicate an appreciably different date, or
otherwise divergent principles of Doric design). The metopes of the
frieze were decorated with rosettes rather than conventional figure
sculpture. There was a splendidly elaborate *sima*, or gutter, with a
continuous maeander pattern on its base, and a series of acanthus
scrolls between lion-head water spouts, all beautifully and flowingly
carved in Pentelic marble.

Behind the colonnade the decoration is unusually elaborate. The
circular wall is decorated with a moulded base, unusual in Doric
architecture. More striking and even more unusual is the elaborate
string-course running above the orthostats. This is moulded, and given
carved decoration, lotus bud and palmettes below, astragal and ovolo
above. This does not have the strict simplicity of, say, the carved
decoration of the Erechtheion at Athens – there are fussy tendrils
between the lotus and the palmettes – but it is exquisitely done, though
distinctly Ionic in flavour. At the top of the wall the crown is decorated
with a maeander pattern, picking up the details of the maeander on the
sima outside, though here surmounting an ovolo; there is another

maeander, at the same level, at the back of the frieze. Between these sections the ceiling is formed from a series of slabs, carved on the underside with a coffering system; there are no supporting beams. The coffers are unusually deep, and in their centre are full, luxuriant flowers. Finally, behind the ramp, the wall is pierced by the door into the *cella*. This has a surround of decorated pilasters, with inset panels edged with carved mouldings and a rosette at the top; the capital is formed with lotus and palmette and ovolo, recalling the pattern of the string-course. All this is of an elaboration and intricacy quite foreign to the normally severe Doric order.

Even so, it serves only as a prelude to the interior. The floor rested on the maze section of the circular foundations already described. By the wall was a circle of stone slabs. Then came a ring of 14 Corinthian columns, the number showing that their position was not related to that of the outer columns. There was a stone ceiling between them and the wall, at the same level as the outer ceiling, and with an even deeper coffer pattern, a single row this time but with square coffers, the angle between the edges of the coffers being filled with an acanthus scroll. There was a new pattern along the inner edge of this section of ceiling, a 'wave' motif, a series of successive spirals. Within this Corinthian colonnade the floor was made up of a compass-drawn pattern, executed in black limestone from Argos and Pentelic marble. According to Pausanias the walls of the *cella* were decorated with a painting by Pausias showing Eros with a lyre instead of his usual bow and arrows, and another painting by the same artist showing Drunkenness holding a wine glass 'through which you can see a woman's face'. There is no evidence for the ceiling over the central section, which was presumably of wood. There is no reason to suppose that it was not horizontal.

Whatever the form of the ceiling, the exterior profile of the roof is certain. It rose in a single continuous slope like a flat cone to the centre point, where it was surmounted by a tall elaborate *acroterion* or finial, based on the pattern of the acanthus plant and scroll. Surviving tiles show how the roof lines radiated from this point. Earlier interpretations and restorations, such as those displayed in the Museum, which show a roof in two sections, a higher inner section supported on an upward extension of the *cella* wall, possibly forming a clerestory, and a lower, pent-roof section, are not substantiated by the evidence of the surviving remains.

The exact purpose of this building has been much debated. Its central importance is clearly demonstrated by the lavishness of its decoration, and by its position at the heart of the sanctuary, so close to the Temple and the Abaton. Circular buildings are found in the sanctuaries of Athena at Delphi (the Tholos) and at Olympia (the Philippeion), though it is by no means demonstrable that their function was the same, and they do not have the same special name as the Epidaurian building, the Thymele. Another Epidaurian peculiarity which requires explanation is the extraordinary arrangement of the inner foundations. Clearly this had a special function but there is no evidence for what this was. A favourite popular explanation is that the maze housed the sacred snakes, though it is unlikely that snakes would have tolerated the perpetual darkness of the outer two rings, and it is difficult to see the reason for the maze. Much more likely is a ritual purpose, connected with particular forms of sacrifice to the dead, to the heroes. The Asklepieion at Athens does not have a circular building, but it does have a pit, which may have fulfilled the same ritual need.

So the building probably reflects the dual status of Asklepios, which authors such as Cicero, writing long after the development of the sanctuary at Epidauros, still clearly appreciated, of a man who lived and died, and who was then promoted to divine form as a god. The Temple with its cult statue clearly and obviously honours Asklepios as a god. The Thymele, not a temple, different in form from a temple but as splendid architecturally and as prominent as the Temple in the central group of buildings, reflects the other aspect. Asklepios had

9 The late fortification wall, composed of material re-used from destroyed buildings

several burial places as a man. One of these was at Epidauros. The Thymele marks this, its conical roof rising like a tumulus over a burial chamber.[39]

Pausanias tells us that the architect was Polykleitos. Unlike the inscriptions for the Temple that for the Thymele does not give the architect's name. Polykleitos was a famous sculptor who lived at Argos in the second half of the fifth century BC, and died long before the Thymele was designed. He cannot possibly have been the architect, though as Pausanias in no way qualifies the name it seems he must have believed this was the famous Polykleitos. The usual solution is to propose that Pausanias is here confused with another Polykleitos, an architect rather than a sculptor, who also designed the Theatre and who was possibly a grandson of Polykleitos the sculptor. This is possible, but since the Thymele is adorned with lavish carved decoration, and the Theatre was famous for its proportions (an aspect much stressed in the sculpture of Polykleitos) it is perhaps more likely that we have here a simple misattribution, which may have been generally accepted by Pausanias' time.

The Abaton

The third major building in the central part of the sanctuary is the Abaton (15), situated immediately to the north of and very close to the Temple, which it faces, extending beyond it to the west. Immediately at its east side is an earlier building (11), two rooms and a portico, going back at least to the middle of the fifth century, and probably functioning as a bath building. It is adjacent to a well, 17 m deep, and giving access to a constant water supply, belonging to the early period of the sanctuary, but subsequently included within the Abaton. Behind this bath building is a confused series of Roman walls and foundations, which once continued the bathing function of this part of the sanctuary into the second century AD. These are the Baths of Antoninus, mentioned by Pausanias as the gift of the mysterious Roman Senator. Tiles for this building are stamped with Antoninus' name.

The Abaton building is close to the Temple, partly perhaps because the ground slopes away here to the west and north, but possibly also to achieve proximity with the god. It was, of course, in this building that the sick slept so that they could be visited by the god and healed during their sleep.

The Abaton is essentially a stoa or portico, open to the south, that is, facing the Temple. It is Ionic, 38.07 m long × 9.42 m wide. To the east it was built against the small fifth-century building. At the back the ground slopes away steeply, so that the rear wall has to rest on foundations which are 4.85 m deep. It had a façade of sixteen Ionic columns; a central row of columns with twice the spacing between them carried the line of the ridge.

The rite of incubation (see page 19) in the Abaton is an essential element in the cult of Asklepios, and it is to be supposed therefore that the building belongs to the earliest phase of development. One cannot be altogether confident of this; the ritual, presumably, had been performed from the first moment Asklepios was established here as a healing god. This (as we have seen, page 25) may have been a function of Building E, and that could have continued since the building was preserved into the fourth century. Alternatively the sick may have slept in the open air, no hardship in a Greek summer. Certainly it can have been no long time before the Abaton was constructed.

It was later doubled in size, being extended to the west. Here the ground slopes away, and heavy substructures were necessary giving a basement with a central row of piers under the inner colonnade. The spaces between the outer columns were closed with a balustrade. The date of this extension is not certain, since its architectural forms are derived from the earlier part and are not a clear indication of date. It is usually assumed that it is Roman, but if so it is built in a technique different from that of the other Roman buildings. Given the need to harmonize with the earlier part, this is not an insuperable objection to a Roman date, but the extension could be of the Hellenistic age.

Beyond the Thymele and the Abaton the ground slopes down, away from the centre of the sanctuary. There are other important buildings in the central area but it is sensible to investigate the lesser structures in this lower area first.

The west end of the extended Abaton coincides with another section of the late fortifications (plate 9), which here turn a corner and pass to the south of the Thymele. Beyond this line, to the west, are more Roman structures (15A). Further still is the well shaft of a fountain house (16), long and narrow, measuring 14 m by 1m. It is surrounded by an outer foundation which Kavvadias suggested supported a roofed superstructure. If so, this may well be the fountain house, mentioned by Pausanias in this area as having a particularly fine roof, of which, of course, all trace has gone. Similar shafts occur at the waterworks of Perachora,[40] near Corinth, probably of about 300 BC. The shape is there explained by the probability that they were designed for lifting machinery in the form of a chain of buckets turning over a wheel. There is no good evidence for this type of apparatus at an earlier date in Greece, and it is likely to be an introduction from the Near East, after Alexander's conquests. If so, it is difficult to relate this fountain to inscriptions which refer to the building of a fountain earlier in the fourth century.

To the north of this, and well away from the central area, are some Roman buildings and a large water storage cistern (17) dug into the ground, its walls lined with masonry. What appear to be buttresses supporting this lining are the remains of transverse arches which would once have supported a roof. There is another cistern of similar size and construction outside the present archaeological zone, by the side of the track which leads towards the Maleatas sanctuary. The date of these is uncertain, but the form of cistern with a roof supported on transverse arches is Hellenistic, being found, for example, in the third-century-BC cistern in front of the Theatre at Delos. A little to the north-west of cistern (17) is a very large Roman building (17A). It consists of a tower (plate 10), in brick and rubble, of massive construction, largely collapsed on its north-west side. Very noticeably, brick has been used by itself in the corners to strengthen the construction. There is a large area of courtyard and rooms to the west of this, now very overgrown and inadequately planned. These buildings obviously housed an important function, presumably an extension of the ritual and cult of the sanctuary which may have been devoted to the Egyptian goddess Isis.

To the south of the fountain house (16) is a group of rooms (18) excavated by Kavvadias very shortly before he died and not adequately published. They are usually described as the Palaistra. Two long narrow halls to the north are followed by another room at the north-east corner of an open area, on a slightly different alignment. The complex is linked to the Stadium (30) by a vaulted passageway: it is unfortunate that at present the perimeter fence of the archaeological zone comes between the group of rooms and the Stadium (and that the passageway is consequently obstructed) since it is clear that the two are very closely associated. The rooms can be identified as the Gymnasium; the place of exercise is attested in an inscription. Gymnasia are found similarly in direct relationship with stadia at, for example, Priene. It is more logical that the Gymnasium is here rather than in the splendid Banqueting Hall (26), identified on inadequate grounds as the Gymnasium by Kavvadias, an identification which has been accepted subsequently without question, and which therefore still confusingly appears on the monument itself and in the Museum. The recent study of the Stadium by Roberto Patrucco dismisses (18) as Roman, without giving any support to this idea. A vaulted passage in the Stadium at Nemea, similar to the one here, is now definitely dated to around 320 BC.

Returning past the Thymele, the late fortification wall crosses over

10 The Roman building 17A; brick-faced concrete

11 A semi-circular exedra and rectangular statue-base by Building E

the foundations of two fourth-century buildings, described as 'ancillary' (**19**) and a 'workshop' (**20**). Possibly one was the workshop whose construction is accounted for in the same inscription as the Temple of Asklepios, in which the gold and ivory cult statue was made (like the 'workshop of Pheidias' at Olympia) and justifiably well built for reasons of security. Building (**20**), however, had an open stoa along one side, and may have been intended as a public building.

Monuments

The area around – and particularly in front of – the Temple of Asklepios was the most favoured position for setting up monuments. The chief official inscriptions, building accounts and the stelai recording the miraculous cures came from this region. The appearance of the sanctuary in antiquity must have been profoundly influenced by these various monuments, for which the buildings acted as a backcloth. Of the different categories, the stone benches, the exedrai (plate 11), have been least affected by the passage of time. Many of them survive in their original positions: those by the south side of the Temple in front of the Thymele, and (as has been noted already) the line of them in the central area which helps define that space and relates it to the Altar of Asklepios. Because of their good condition it is still possible to visualize the original appearance of the sanctuary in antiquity, and the seats still – as then – provide a pleasant view of the comings and goings of present-day visitors. The majority of these benches are semicircular in plan, with raised backs. There is an example by the Temple of Asklepios of a rectangular bench which had a slab seat, now missing, resting on slab feet decorated in the form of conventional lion's paws.

Other monuments have not survived so well. The inscribed stelai, massive slabs of stone raised up on bases, have been removed; the historical importance of the texts they carry is too great to be left exposed to the elements and they are now in the Museum, where the best preserved are on public display. Statues also have entirely disappeared, though a headless herm (a conventional monument of Hermes) has been replaced in front of Building E (**22**). A few statues survived in fragmentary state to be removed to the safety of the Museum, but they are not enough to give a fair impression of what once was there. There must have been bronze statue groups, some of them equestrian. Inscriptions on some of the bases recording statues of Macedonian kings and Roman emperors indicate the type of material irretrievably lost. Only some bases remain, mute visual reminders of our loss. Some of these are not without interest in their own right; they may be finely constructed, usually from blocks of hard grey limestone, and given decoration of architectural type, raised panels and mouldings. Others of interest include one triangular-shaped base (plate 12), decorated to recall the prow of a ship, and another immediately outside the front of the Temple of Asklepios by the northern corner of its ramp. The latter has a curious shape (plate 13): a hole on its top surface set in the impression of the right foot of the bronze statue once attached to it, through which water was made to flow, so that the statue acted as a fountain, perhaps facilitating a final ritual purification before one entered the Temple.

Building E and adjacent structures

To the east of the square Altar of Apollo (**21**) is the building labelled E on Kavvadias' plan (here **22**); its ancient name is quite unknown, and most accounts of the sanctuary have retained this label for it. It was in this area that the earliest inscribed dedications (on bronze vases) were found, associated with ash and other debris cleared out from sacrifices, presumably those made on the adjacent square altar. These dedications are more likely to date from the early fifth century than any remoter period; and it is quite clear that the deposit in which they were

12 Ship's prow statue-base

found was laid down before Building E was constructed, probably in
the second part of the fifth century BC.

The building itself consists of a courtyard, about 15 × 12 m,
originally open to the west, that is, facing the square altar (21). On the
east and north sides of the courtyard were porticos consisting of a
screen wall decorated with engaged Ionic half columns. These were of
the typically Peloponnesian type, equivalent to full columns with 20
flutes, in contradistinction to the east Greek type, which has 24. There
was a long narrow room on the south side. The court itself was divided
into two parts by a low support wall which runs in an irregular fashion
from north-west to south-east. There was a small, shrine-like room at
the west end of the north wing, and another, possibly a shrine and an
altar, to the south of it. This west side was closed, in Hellenistic times,
with the construction of a portico whose solid limestone foundations
can be clearly distinguished from the tufa of the earlier building.

One can only guess at the purpose of this building; since it was
preserved as the sanctuary grew, and as, in a sense, the later major
buildings were arranged to take account of it and its position, it was
obviously important. One tenable suggestion is that it was the original
cult building for Asklepios, containing altar, shrine and incubation
room. This is not unlikely, and is perhaps preferable to assigning one
distinct function to the building. The small room and the structure on
the west destroyed by the later portico served as temple and altar, the

13 Statue-base of the bronze figure fountain

long room on the south side perhaps as the Abaton, while the porticos and courtyard have the functions later taken into the Banqueting Hall. Once these functions were dispersed, the building may have been preserved out of respect. But the building does not seem to have been deeply venerable; the ash layer is probably debris spread from the square altar and does not really imply that this precise spot was a hallowed place of sacrifice; and the building itself does not really give any indication of what the ritual function was. It may be connected with the cult of Apollo rather than Asklepios, particularly as there is no temple of Apollo in the lower sanctuary.

Beyond Building E is another temple (23) dedicated to Artemis. It seems to have been built around 330 BC, that is, in the second phase of the main development. Artemis is Apollo's twin sister, and the presence of her temple in the lower rather than the upper sanctuary shows that the Apolline interest was still maintained. There is earlier evidence for her cult on an inscription[41] but not for an earlier temple; an earlier altar may be concealed on the south side of the present altar.

The temple itself was small, 13.38 × 9.42 m at the top of the foundations (figures 13 and 14). Only a small gap separates it from Building E. Its back wall, not relieved with columns, is close to the front alignment of that building, its Doric façade, of six columns, is concealed from the area round the Temple of Asklepios by Building E; it does not, therefore, have any significant visual relationship with that Temple or the Thymele. Instead, it had its own area, approached from behind Building E.

The base had three steps which ran all round the building, although the colonnade, which has disappeared entirely, was restricted to the façade. There is the usual approach ramp at the front. A paved area extends around and beyond the ramp up to the altar, here placed in direct alignment with the axis of the Temple. The columns of the façade were made from poros and stuccoed. Roux[42] calculates column height, with the capital, at 4 to 4.15 m, that is about seven times the lower diameter. There was a normal triglyph and metope frieze extending along the *cella* walls as well as over the colonnade. There was a marble *sima*, decorated with scroll patterns, but with the spouts in the form of wild boars' heads, rather than the usual lions' heads, an appropriate motif for Artemis the huntress. The interior of the *cella* measured 7.50 × 6.96 m only; nevertheless, like the other temples it contained an inner colonnade, structurally unnecessary, and so decorative in function. Here there are definite fragments of Corinthian capitals. The colonnades were set at a space of one floor slab from the side walls, restricting the free space, but against the end wall. The floor of the western half of the *cella* was polished smooth,

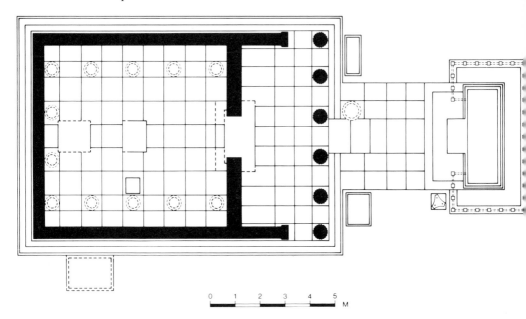

13 The Temple of Artemis: plan (*after G. Roux*)

while the front half had a stippled surface; presumably only the front half was normally accessible. Roux suggests a barrier between the two halves; he places the cult statue on a base at the centre of the *cella*, and a stone table on another base against the rear colonnade.

The altar was splendid and substantial. It has a stepped base 4.5 × 3.5 m. The altar itself occupied the eastern part. It must have had a moulded course at the bottom, of which nothing survives. Over this the main body was constructed from six grey limestone orthostat blocks 0.60 m high, all of which, rather surprisingly, survive. There would have been a further crowning moulding which has totally disappeared. Around the altar and outside its base was a line of poros blocks with square holes cut in their upper surface to hold the upright posts of a fence. The cuttings for these are shallow, so they are likely to have been stone.

Thirty metres to the east of the temple, beyond the altar, is a rectangular limestone base (**24**) 4.90 × 7.44 m with two steps. The upper surface has the marks of a wall on it, half the width of the steps (0.235 m instead of 0.52 m) but reinforced with pilasters at the corners, the centres of the long sides, and at either side of openings in the centre of each end. There is a ramp at the eastern end and presumably once another at the western opening. A narrow line of

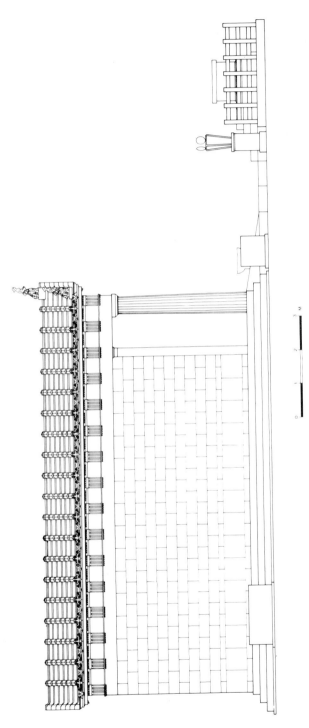

14 The Temple of Artemis: elevation (*after G. Roux*)

upright slabs divided the interior into two. There is a rectangular base in the eastern part, badly damaged, which probably supported an altar. The structure is unlikely to have been roofed; it forms a screen with entrances at east and west. Roux[43] compares it with the altar of the twelve gods at Athens: the architectural arrangement recalls even more forcibly the altar of Augustan Peace at Rome, which was surely based on Greek altar screens of this type. Masons' marks in the form of letters date the structure to the main fourth-century period of development. It is not possible to deduce the cult, whether a single or double one, to which it was dedicated.

To the south-east of the Temple of Artemis and its Altar is a courtyard building (25), its door facing onto an open space at the side of the Temple. It has rooms of varying size all round the central court, the largest occupying the whole of the north side. It was originally identified by Kavvadias as the portico given to the sanctuary by the Thracian Kotys but, at least in its present form, it belongs to the Roman period, and it is safer to identify as Kotys' Portico the building (3) on the north side of the central area. Nevertheless, this is an interesting building. Particularly noticeable are the lines of well-carved stone benches in the courtyard. Though the construction of the walls with mortared rubble is obviously Roman it includes on the outside selected stones of the Greek period, easily recognized by their characteristic rows of chisel-mark decoration (some, in error, are set the wrong way round). The foundations also seem solid, and the possibility should be borne in mind that this, like so much Roman work, may be reconstruction rather than a totally new building. Even so, the view of the Temple of Artemis and the spectacular propylon of the building to the south would be much improved if this area had been empty space.

The structure to the south (26) is another courtyard building, but this time undoubtedly of Greek date – probably the early Hellenistic period, about 300 BC. It measures 75.36 × 69.535 m externally, not including the imposing entrance which projects from the western end of its north side, facing the Temple of Artemis. This porch was the first part of the building to be excavated, and it was originally published by Kavvadias in his *Fouilles d'Epidaure* as an isolated structure in its own right, interpreted as a propylon entrance to the whole sanctuary. It was only when the area to the south was excavated that it was found to be joined, at its centre, to the outer wall of the courtyard building, to which it formed the principal entrance. Unfortunately R. Martienssen, in his interesting and valuable book on the spatial arrangements of Greek sanctuaries, based his interpretation of Epidauros on this erroneous preliminary report. His comments on the appearance of the

14 Ramp approach to the Banqueting Hall

sanctuary from this building entrance are a good analysis of what
would have been visible but bear no relation to the actual spatial
rhythm related to the true Propylon to the north.

This entrance structure consists of a raised platform 18.12 × 10.91 m
approached by the inevitable ramp on its north side, but otherwise
with three steps all round. Across the front were six Doric columns
with a wider central intercolumnar space. There were four columns at
each side. Behind this a narrow waist, 8.91 m wide × 2.47 m. deep,
links the platform to the main building. There were walls on either side
of this, with outward turned *antae* in line with the rear columns of the
platform. In the same line, but this time between the *antae*, were two
more columns, possibly Ionic. The entrance doors are at the back of
this section, at the line of the outer wall of the main building. The
general arrangement, with the restricted section behind a wide façade,
recalls the north Propylon; not exactly the same, but close enough for
the architecture to be related. It is a spectacular flourish to the
building.

At the centre of the main building is the square courtyard 33.12 ×
33.12 m with sixteen Doric columns on each of its four sides, the
colonnade on the north side being doubled internally. This courtyard
was originally a clear open space but as it survives it is confused and
obscured by a theatre-like Roman structure of mortared brick,
generally described as an odeion or music-hall. The Roman work

15 Small dining-rooms in the Banqueting Hall

incorporates several of the original Doric columns in its structure, and extends in places into the area behind the colonnade, originally roofed; clearly the roof had to be destroyed, if it was not already ruinous, to make way for this. Behind the original colonnade there were rooms on all four sides. On each side there is one substantial, or fairly substantial room. The largest is that on the south 54.085 × 12.85 m, which once had a row of nine columns, spaced at 5.477 m to support the roof. In the corners, on each side, are two rooms 6.34 × 6.34 m, with off-centre doors (plate 15). There were two similar rooms next to these, but opening, through a porch, into the south colonnade of the courtyard. Of these, that on the west side is in its original state, but that on the east was converted into a subsidiary entrance by having a doorway with a threshold cut in its outer wall, presumably at the same time as the Roman Theatre, which obstructs access to this south side, was built.

On the north side is a long (38.55 m) narrow (6.03 m) hall, with three doorways from the court and a central square projection in its outer wall. The west side has a suite of smallish rooms running from the side of the main entrance passage, some rectangular, some square, and then a larger room 19.87 × 7.98 m with three inner columns occupying the space between these and the rooms of the south-west corner already described. Finally, the east side has a hall 24.38 × 7.98 m, with an inner colonnade of six supports and a pair of small square rooms at either end, and three rectangular rooms at the north. It is this east hall which preserves the best evidence for the original function of this building.

Structures with large central colonnaded courts attached to sanctuaries are usually regarded as places of physical exercise (gymnasium) or for wrestling (*palaistrai*). This example at Epidauros, following Kavvadias' interpretation, is invariably described as a gymnasium. Certainly the Stadium and the literary evidence are clear proof that athletic exercise formed part of Epidaurian activities. The practices of the gymnasium required considerable space (the Gymnasium at Olympia, for example, measures over 220 m on its long side) and though the Epidaurian building is large it does not approach that scale. The spectacular entrance suggests that this building is more than a mere exercise yard, a view confirmed by the numerous rooms. Still surviving against the outer wall of the eastern hall are several stone supports with dowel holes in their upper surfaces. The purpose of the dowels was to secure wooden planks fitted from one support to the next. They are set too high (0.45 m) to hold a conventional bench running along the wall, the usual interpretation of their function. Marks on the wall, and the position of one support, clearly show that some planks projected out into the width of the room, and were not restricted to a single line along the wall. The spacing of the surviving supports, and traces of those now removed, demonstrate that each section was of the right length (about 1.8 m) for a couch. The 'couches' were arranged to form squares, an arrangement which was also certainly found in the six rooms in the south-east and south-west corners, each 6.34 m square. Rooms of similar dimensions to these, and with clear evidence for the existence of couches, are found in other sanctuaries (for example, at Brauron in Attica and at Perachora). In these square rooms each side wall has three couches placed along its length, together with the feet of one couch by an adjacent wall. There is thus space for twelve couches, but one has to be omitted to allow for the entrance. Since this entrance space has room for one couch to one side, but for a couch plus the foot of a couch on the other, it cannot be at the centre of a side; the off-centre doors of the six rooms prove that they contained couches. The largest hall, on the south side, also preserves one solitary couch support and here, again, though this has been interpreted as evidence for a continuous bench along the outer wall, it was probably part of a system of couches arranged in squares, as in the east hall. It is likely that the largest of the rooms on the west side functioned in the same way, but there is now no evidence for this and the room itself was affected by the later alterations. There is a very similar, but smaller, courtyard building with the remains of couches in small select rooms as well as larger halls in a sanctuary at Troizen, the next important state to the east of Epidauros, which has been identified as an Asklepieion.

These couches could have functioned as beds, but there is no reason to identify this building as another Abaton for the ritual of incubation; that was properly and more suitably restricted to the building near the Temple and Thymele. Couches were required by the Greeks for dining since they reclined rather than sat to table. This Epidaurian building is therefore a *hestiatorion* or Banqueting Hall (the Greek term survives on inscriptions from Delos and elsewhere). Whether the courtyard, at least, could also have functioned as a gymnasium remains problematical. The provision for water supplies which Delorme[44] notes in the north-west rooms may indicate gymnastic functions, with the necessary facilities for bathing and washing, but other buildings with dining-rooms and couches (at Perachora, and the Sanctuary of Asklepios at Corinth) also have elaborate arrangements for water supplies. The Troizen building has substantial drainage – presumably the floors would require swilling down – and this is also found in the large dining-rooms of the palace at Vergina in Macedon. Often the floors of these dining-rooms are paved in small pebbles set in cement – Perachora is an example. The floors of our building are not now visible, but the original excavation report seems to suggest that they were also of pebble-cement. As we have seen, a gymnasium was provided at Epidauros, and is mentioned in a very fragmentary and 'otherwise uninformative' inscription[45] but this should be located at the courtyard building by the side of the Stadium.

The walls of the Banqueting Hall survive only to orthostat height. They are of grey limestone. There are no traces of an ashlar superstructure and it is more likely that it was of mud-brick, an economy also found in the palace at Vergina. This does not mean, then, that the building was unimportant. Its size, the splendid entrance, the large colonnaded court with stone Doric columns, the survival of good-quality decoration and (from somewhere in the interior) small Ionic half columns with calyx voluces, similar to the Ionic half columns in the palace at Vergina, attest to its considerable significance.

It is generally assumed that the Banqueting Hall had fallen into disrepair and had been abandoned when, in Roman times, the porch was converted into a temple of Hygieia (Health) and the theatre-like structure erected in the courtyard (plate 16). This is difficult to accept. The fact that the columns of the courtyard are incorporated into the Roman structure cannot have greatly facilitated its building, and it would have been easier to have built on an unencumbered site. The

16 Banqueting Hall: the Roman theatre structure, incorporating the original courtyard columns

fact that the stone footings to the walls of the earlier Greek building are still standing now obviously means they were there in the Roman period. If the building had been tumbled ruins the debris would have impeded access to the Theatre quite seriously. The implication is that the original building survived, even if parts had to be altered or removed to accommodate the Roman construction. In general the original rooms are not much altered and could well have continued their function as banqueting rooms, for feasting still played an important part in the ritual. The Roman structure is much smaller than the great Greek Theatre, and cannot have usurped the role of that building, nor can its size be explained, as has been attempted, by a reduced scale of activities in Roman times leading to the abandonment of the Theatre, since all the other evidence suggests an increased scale of activity, at least at the time that the Roman building was constructed. Nor can it be explained by the difference of form between the Greek and Roman Theatre, since here too we have a total difference of scale, and elsewhere no difficulty was found in adapting Greek theatres to Roman practice. To call this Roman structure an odeion or music-hall is merely to apply a conventional name for these small theatre-like buildings. A possible explanation is that the original courtyard was the location for some solemn religious ritual with a dramatic content; or at least that some such ritual developed, and that the Roman construction was put up for the greater convenience of the spectators. It may be that such a ritual was performed by the bards, the *aoidoi*, who are mentioned in the inscription which details the proper sacrifices, as receiving a special portion of the sacrificial meat; so this building could be not only the place where they performed, but where, along with the other named recipients of the sacred meat, the *hiaromnamones* and the guards, they feasted.

To the south is another courtyard building (**27**), with walls similar in construction, limestone footings and orthostats with, presumably, unbaked brick superstructure. It is described as a bath building.[46] The inner arrangement is not now possible to make out. It appears to belong to the main development of the sanctuary, but probably to its final, third-century phase. Its identification is supported by the discovery of facilities for water supply and disposal. An inscription added to the side of the stone which carries the Thymele accounts, but in a later style of lettering, seems to refer to the construction of a *Balaneion* or bath building, though the word is not completely preserved. The limestone construction of Building (**27**) and the lettering style of the inscription both belong to the same final phase of the main construction.

The Katagogion (*Hostel Building*)

This structure lies between the central cluster of buildings and the Theatre (see figure 4). It is a large building, 76.3 m square, divided internally into four courtyards, each surrounded with rooms. Two courtyards had direct access from outside, and from each there was a doorway through to one of the other courts. There were probably two storeys.

The building was largely utilitarian, though on a grand scale, and without any specific cult function. It provided living accommodation, necessary at a sanctuary which was some distance from the city. It does not have the same formal arrangement as the Banqueting Hall, which, of course, did have a function in the ritual of the sanctuary. The rooms vary in size, and there are no large halls. Nevertheless some of the doorways seem to have been off-centre, so that the provision of couches is possible, though these must have been for sleeping as well as feasting. It is situated away from the centre of the sanctuary, so that the possibility has to be considered that it was outside the boundary, the *peribolos*. This is unlikely: in that case the Theatre, which is even further away, would also have had to have been outside, but Pausanias distinctly implies that it was within the sanctuary. Some sanctuaries designated quite clearly the most sacred area, where normally worshippers would not be allowed to sleep except for ritual purposes, and where they might be prohibited from eating and drinking, and an ancillary or less sacred area where such activities were permitted. On the Athenian Acropolis, for example, it seems that a dining-room was provided in the north-west wing of the Propylaia, outside the formal gateway, and at Perachora the dining-rooms are away from the area of temple and altar. At Epidauros there is no demarcation. All came within the sacred grove.

The term *katagogion* is nowhere attested for this building, for which no certain building inscription survives, but is commonly applied by modern archaeologists to accommodation buildings of this type. Other inscriptions from Epidauros refer to comparable accommodation (but in these cases definitely outside the sanctuary) – dwelling houses (*skanamata*) on Mt Kyon. There is no reason to suppose that there was any significant difference in function, though there is possibly a difference in the status of the persons allowed to use the various buildings, those in the sanctuary being reserved for priests, officials and other privileged worshippers. Nor is there any real reason to postulate a different nomenclature for the various buildings, so *katagogion* may not be the correct name. The date for them all seems to be in the final phase of the main development, that is the first part of the third century BC. The Hostel Building was later damaged, and its original arrangements are in part obscured, particularly on the east side.

The Theatre

As we have seen, the cult of Asklepios included contests, artistic and athletic, which were a common feature of Greek religious practice. There is good evidence that these were already established before the great architectural development of the sanctuary. The artistic contests included singing and recitation – the art of the Rhapsode – and other music. Presumably these contests were held in the sanctuary but without any buildings or structures being necessary for them. Whether they included, at this stage, anything resembling dramatic performances is uncertain, but forms of sacred drama were produced in various parts of Greece, and in the fifth century BC were more likely than not performed without any theatre building as such.

The stone Theatre which was subsequently built at Epidauros (plate 17) is justly the sanctuary's most famous structure; not only is it the only building which is at all well preserved, but it has a beauty and

17 The Theatre

symmetry which was praised in antiquity by Pausanias. It is obviously part of the main development of the sanctuary, when Asklepios was provided with all the buildings proper to his status and required for his cult. The exact period of its construction is less certain but important, not only for the history of the sanctuary, but of the general development of the Greek theatre.

Pausanias tells us that the architect was Polykleitos, whom he also considered to be the architect of the Thymele. As we have seen, the Thymele was next in sequence to the Temple, as part of the first phase of construction. The Theatre would appear therefore to be associated with the Thymele, even if, accepting the long-drawn out work on the latter, we place the building of the Theatre at the end of this phase. So Alison Burford puts it at 360 BC or thereabouts,[47] its construction taking some time and so forming a link between the first and second phases. On the other hand, if Pausanias believed that Polykleitos was the famous Argive sculptor (and, as we have seen with the Thymele, since he does not qualify the name in any way it must be presumed that this was so) he is clearly in error. Thus it may be that the two structures were not by the same architect at all (particularly if we discard the concept of a younger Polykleitos) and, therefore, there need be no chronological link between them.

In their exhaustive study of this Theatre, A. von Gerkan and W. Müller-Wiener propose basically a later date, at the very end of the fourth century or the early third century BC, with subsequent alterations. Their view is based partly on the form of the few examples of architectural mouldings and other decoration which have survived, and also on the general proposition that this carefully planned and sophisticated structure should be later than the transformation of the stone theatre of Dionysos at Athens, which occurred around 340 BC. There is one fragmentary inscription, however, not known to von Gerkan and Müller-Wiener, which refers to the construction of the Theatre. This has been published by Miss Burford.[48] The letter style of this relates it to the building inscription concerned with the construction of the Temple of Artemis, that is, some time after 330 BC, and one individual, Kleidikos, is mentioned, as member and secretary of the board respectively in that inscription and the Theatre inscription. The latter inscription refers to payment for the seats so construction was presumably well under way. Even so, a start as early as 360, and before both the Temple of Artemis and the Theatre at Athens, seems improbable, and it is preferable to assign the Theatre to the second phase of construction, after the peace imposed on the Greek world by Philip of Macedon and the stimulus of Alexander's conquests; that is, to the last part of the fourth century BC.

The Theatre is not only the best-preserved building at Epidauros but one of the best preserved of all Greek theatres although it is not complete. The extremities of the curved auditorium had partly fallen, taking with them some of the seats, but the walls have been put back now, and the missing seats made good. More serious is the loss of the stage building, reduced in a manner more typical of Epidauros to bare foundations. The contrast shows the fortuitous nature of the Theatre's preservation; the auditorium, in the hollow of the hillside, must have filled with earth, covering the seats completely until they were excavated in the nineteenth century, while the stage building remained exposed until robbed completely of its superstructure. It would have been most interesting to know when this silting up of the auditorium took place, whether it was gradual, or the result of a landslip at some precise moment and, if so, when this was. The silt must have contained the evidence but it was all shovelled away in the nineteenth century. Enough of the stage building survives to show the general arrangement of a narrow elevated stage with slight projections at either end, almost tangential to the central circular *orchestra*, or dancing floor, and extending up to the point where the auditorium begins. A ramp led onto the stage at either side. Immediately behind the stage was a rectangular room with supports for an interior colonnade. This room must have risen high enough to provide a backcloth, as it were, to the stage with the three doors, which are conventional in Greek stage buildings, giving access to the stage itself. To either side the stage building is linked to the auditorium support wall by an open structure, decorated with pilasters and carrying an Ionic entablature. Each has two openings, one being to the passageway (*parodos*) which leads to the *orchestra*, the other to the ramp which leads onto the stage. At a later period additional rooms were constructed behind the ramps, and there are general traces of repairs after substantial damage.

The existence from the beginning of this stage building is a clear indication that this Theatre was intended for the performance of plays in the conventional form established by the Athenian drama of the fifth century BC. The Theatre therefore has the conventional *orchestra* where the dramatic chorus performed and danced their choral odes. It is slightly over 19.5 m in diameter, with a floor of beaten earth. There is a small circular slab at the centre (though this is not quite the point from which the lines of the steps dividing the seats into blocks radiate). It is commonly supposed that it supported an altar, though von Gerkan thinks it too small, and suggests rather that it is just a marker for the central point. It is not clear why a marker should be required. At the perimeter of the *orchestra* is a slabbed drainage channel, essential to prevent the rain water descending from the auditorium washing over the *orchestra* floor.

18 The Stadium, with the vaulted passage

The auditorium is in two parts, the lower with 34 rows of seats (the bottom and top rows being superior, with carved backs, the remainder backless benches of the usual sort) while the upper part has 21 rows of seats, only the lower one of which has backs. The two parts are separated by a walkway, and are divided into wedges, each of about 18°–19°, by lines of steps, twice as many in the upper part. As in the theatres at Corinth and Argos (but differing in this characteristic from most other Greek theatres) there is a line of steps rather than a wedge of seats at the centre. The angle of elevation is 26° or a little over. The seats and other stonework (supporting walls, etc.) are of hard local limestone. Some parts (some seats, and the separating walkways) use the pinkish limestone similar to that being quarried at present near the village of Ligourio.

In their investigation of the Theatre, von Gerkan and Müller-Wiener found blocks with a rounded top rather like that on the parapet which crowns the side walls of the auditorium, but not exactly the same, and for which there is no obvious place in the Theatre as it is preserved. They suggested that the blocks came from the top of a wall which once existed behind the lower part of the auditorium, and that therefore the auditorium was built in two distinct phases: an initial phase, when it was small and restricted to the lower section, and a later one, when it was enlarged by the addition of the upper part, the wall at the back of the lower part being then removed. This proposition seems unlikely for, if a small theatre was initially planned, it would hardly, in this position, require the substantial side walls to retain and support a sufficient area of seating. Architecturally the Theatre makes better sense if planned to include the two parts from the outset and it is significant that there is no distinct change in construction or design between them.

The auditorium provides seating space for 13,000–14,000 people, a capacity that must reflect the number of worshippers who attended the festival – more, but not substantially more than the probable population of Epidauros itself. The majority must have come from Epidauros and the neighbouring towns. The acoustic qualities are, of course, excellent, and are better tested by attending a performance of the modern Epidauros festival than by listening to a single spokesman orating to a coachload of tourists from the centre of the *orchestra*. There is no particular magic of design which creates these excellent acoustical properties; they result from the normal arrangement of the auditorium in the Greek theatre.

The Stadium

Before leaving the main archaeological zone the visitor should see the Museum, which contains so much of the surviving superstructure from the important buildings. The other monuments are outside the main archaeological zone.

The Stadium (**30**) is situated by the car park, and is at present awkwardly separated from the rest of the sanctuary to which it belongs by the old approach road and its own fence. It is not accessible, but can be inspected from outside its surrounding fence (plate 18).

The other kind of contest held in celebration of Asklepios was the athletic. This is attested from the early part of the fifth century BC, for Pindar in his Vth Nemean ode refers to Themistios' victory in the all-in wrestling contest at Epidauros. Epidauros thus takes its place with other sanctuaries where athletics were part of the ritual, activities which developed particularly during the sixth century BC. At that time none of the sanctuaries where athletic contests were held had elaborate structures to accommodate them. A suitable area was marked out, facilities would be provided to ensure proper starting for the races, but the spectators would simply stand to either side of the course, which might be situated so that there were convenient slopes from which they might obtain a satisfactory view.

The Stadium at Epidauros is in what was originally a natural valley or depression, providing a running ground and suitable slopes for the spectators. There is no reason to doubt that it was always in the same locality, which is eminently suitable and close to the centre of the sanctuary, being only some 80 m to the south-west of the Temple, but there is no archaeological evidence for its existence there at an early date. The Stadium is mentioned in the Fountain House inscription,[49] apparently as a point of reference, so probably it was already clearly defined in the fourth century. There are remains of a wall outside the eastern end of the running track which may belong to work carried out at this time, or even earlier.

The main work on the Stadium seems to belong to the latter part of the fourth century BC, though there is evidence for later work also. The Stadium consists of a running track, defined by starting (or finishing) lines at either end, 180.12 m long by 21.51 m wide; the length, equivalent to 600 feet, is the normal one for the running tracks of ancient stadia. The Stadium is banked on both sides, the banking being in part enhanced artificially. Unlike later stadia, but in common with other early examples, the end is squared off, not rounded. This may in fact be retained from an earlier phase, for the stadium at Nemea, dated securely to the last quarter of the fourth century, has a rounded end. At the edge of the running track, at the bottom of the banking, is a shallow stone water channel. At intervals this widens out to form basins, whose edges are rounded to make sure that the water flows through them without hindrance, to prevent the depositing of dirt. From these the athletes could cool themselves; the channels, unlike that round the *orchestra* of the theatre, are not just for drainage purposes. Also along the sides are distance blocks placed at intervals of 100 feet.

The seating on the banks is made from stone blocks, each slightly over a metre in length, that is four feet. An inscription, probably belonging to the later part of the second phase, records the transport of large quantities of stone blocks four feet in length. It seems reasonable to assign these to the Stadium, which thus achieved its definitive form in the second part of the fourth century BC.

There is evidence for later alteration. Part, at least, of the seating on the north side, where some of the actual seats are still preserved at the present day, seems to have been renewed when a passageway was constructed leading directly to the level of the running floor. On the outside this connects with the Gymnasium, making it most unlikely that that was in any sense a construction of the Roman period. Part of the passage is vaulted. The art of keystone vaulting was thoroughly understood by the Macedonians, who used it for many underground structures, including the tombs of, at least, their later kings. Nearer to Epidauros there are vaulted passages leading to the upper part of the auditorium at the Theatre of Sikyon, built when that city was reconstructed on a new site by the Macedonian King Demetrios Poliorketes. R. Patrucco suggests that the passage was constructed in two stages, in which differences of building technique are noticeable, the outer uncovered section being older than the vaulted part, which he dates to the second or first century BC. A date in the third century or even earlier is preferable for the vaulted section, and this has been confirmed by a comparable vaulted passageway dated on secure archaeological evidence to the years around 320 BC recently discovered by Stephen Millar at the Stadium of Nemea.[50] If its outer section is of a different date, it is surely later than the vaulted part.

An inscription, probably of the latter part of the third century BC, records a fine imposed on a contractor in connection with the starting-gate of the Stadium. It is not clear what went wrong, or what work was being carried out. Obviously there was always some arrangement for ensuring a fair start, not perhaps as complex as the early system at Isthmia where wooden gates were simultaneously released by strings, but at least a line to show where the start was. The third-century work probably entailed some embellishment, and possibly the construction of individual openings between posts through which the contestants ran. The system visible at present, with half columns decorating stone piers, is probably later than the third century.

The Maleatas sanctuary

The sanctuary of Apollo Maleatas lies to the east of the lower sanctuary, higher up on the hill slopes (figure 3, plate 19). No doubt in antiquity the two sanctuaries were directly connected; the inscriptions recording the proper sacrifices to Apollo and to Asklepios demonstrate an essential unity. Building work on the upper sanctuary is recorded on inscriptions set up in the lower. There must have been a direct route from the eastern side of the lower sanctuary to the upper, but at present this is blocked by the perimeter fence surrounding the main archaeological zone, the lower sanctuary.

To reach the Maleatas sanctuary the modern visitor has to return along the modern road towards Ligourio. At the first house on the right hand side of this road (leaving the sanctuary) a dirt track branches off to the north. Another track to the right soon leads in a generally easterly direction, passing the perimeter of the main archaeological zone close to the remains of the Propylon. From here the track climbs steadily until it reaches a farm house. Up to this point it is just about passable for cars; beyond the farm it is not. Just before

19 The Maleatas sanctuary

the farm, on the southern side of the track, is the large cistern similar in construction to that in the lower sanctuary (17) but better preserved with some of the crossing arches that supported the roof intact. It may have acted as a header tank to supply water to the sanctuary below, or to some of the dwelling accommodation on Mt Kyon, mentioned in the inscriptions, which must have been in this area.

In the hills, to the south-west of this cistern, is a small isolated temple (Temple L), part of whose structure was re-used in the Christian church by the Propylon. Roux has studied and collected these fragments,[51] and from them restores the building in the unusual form of an Ionic pseudo-peripteral temple. It has the usual ramp at the east end, with an altar in front of it. The platform is higher than normal, consisting of four steps, presumably because the temple is in the Ionic order. The foundations measure 7.96 × 13.53 m. There was a façade of four Ionic columns, in the Peloponnesian form with only twenty flutes to the shaft, and four-sided volute capitals. Behind this façade came a further column on either side, and then the *cella*, extending in width to the stylobate but decorated along its sides with a further five columns, those at the corners being almost but not quite free from the wall, those at the centre being engaged as three-quarter columns against the wall. The columns at the back of the temple are similarly engaged. As usual, despite the small size, there was an internal colonnade on either side and across the back of the *cella*, and this was Corinthian. The temple probably belongs to the very end of the fourth century or the beginning of the third century BC. It is quite impossible to discover the deity to whom it was dedicated. Roux believes it is the Temple of Aphrodite mentioned by Pausanias, but in a description which appears to be related to the main sanctuary, since in the same sentence he mentions the Temple of Artemis, the statue of Epione and the Temple of Themis. If Pausanias' locations are here imprecise, and Temple L is that of Aphrodite, we must assume that a vast area on the western slopes of Kynortion was included within the sanctuary.

The sanctuary of Apollo Maleatas is on the side of the hill overlooking the farm, on the southern side, and beyond Temple L. It is at present completely fenced off and generally inaccessible, though some of the structures can be made out without going in. The most recent excavation work at Epidauros, by B. Lambrinoudakis, is being conducted in this sanctuary, and has produced ample evidence for the early period, before the development of the lower sanctuary, as well as the prehistoric settlement here.

The earliest religious usage centred round an altar of non-monumental form. Nothing of this is now visible. Otherwise, the architectural embellishment of this original sanctuary belongs only to the period when the lower sanctuary was undergoing its main phase of construction; Apollo here is clearly benefiting from the popularity of the off-shoot cult of his son. However, a wall found under the fourth-century temple may belong to a predecessor of the sixth century BC. The main improvement was the construction of a great terrace support wall, the *analamma*; this can be seen from the north side. On it stood a stoa, facing inwards – that is, to the south. The inscription recording the construction of this support wall seems dated by its letter style to about 330 BC.

The temple was situated to the south-west of this on ground which did not require its support. It could therefore be earlier in date, and it is not impossible that it was built at the same time as the Temple of Asklepios. It has not been properly published. It is small, measuring about 8.5 × 14.2 m. There is a ramp at its east end, and steps all round its base. It seems to have been Doric and possibly, as Roux suggests, amphiprostyle, that is, with columns at either end, instead of just at the east end. Clearly it cannot have had columns all round, like the much larger Temple of Asklepios. It had pedimental sculpture in Pentelic marble. The *cella* seems to have opened directly behind the front colonnade, without a porch.

The other structures in this little sanctuary are Roman, and of well-preserved mortared construction. They include a fountain, a large cistern and an elaborate structure with several rooms, on the eastern side of the sanctuary.

Notes

1. She discusses the epigraphy in an article in *BSA* 61 (1966) 254–334.
2. An exception to this is the brief preliminary discussion of the North-East Baths by R. Ginouvès in *BCH* 79 (1955) 141.
3. Burford, *Temple Builders*, 13–35, gives a résumé of Epidaurian history.
4. *Archaeological Reports*, 1978–9 18.
5. The *testimonia* are all included in volume 1 of the fundamental study of Asklepios and his cult, *Asclepius*, by E. J. and L. Edelstein.
6. Greek text: IG IV^2 128.
7. The texts of the dedicatory inscriptions are given in IG IV^2 171–95.
8. IG IV^2 40/41. Words translated between brackets do not survive on the stone as preserved.
9. IG IV^2 47.
10. Pausanias II 27.1.
11. Plato *Ion* 530a.
12. Greek texts: IG IV^2 121–4.
13. Recent excavations summarized: *Archaeological Reports* 1977–8 28, 1978–9 18. Earlier excavations: J. Papadimitriou *Praktika* 1950.
14. Burford, *Temple Builders* 41.
15. L. H. Jeffrey, *Local scripts of Archaic Greece* 180.
16. IG II^2 4960.
17. IG IV^2 94.
18. For this administration, see Burford, *Temple Builders* 120f.
19. Texts, IG IV^2 102–20, supplemented by Burford *BSA* 61 (1966) 254–334.
20. Burford, *Temple Builders* XX.
21. IG IV^2 102 and Burford (*BSA* 61) Inscription I. Translation (in French) in Roux, *L'architecture* 424–32.
22. IG IV^2 118, Burford (*BSA* 61) Inscription II.
23. IG IV^2 103, Burford (*BSA* 61) Inscription VI.
24. *Periocha* of Book XI.
25. Plutarch *Sulla* 12.3; *Pompey* 24.5.
26. Pausanias II 27.7.
27. *Hermes* 1929, 63.
28. *Pausanias Guide to Greece* (Penguin Classics translation) Vol. 1 footnote 153 on page 192.
29. Justin, *Dialogues* 69.3.
30. *Life of Constantine* III 56.
31. *In Helium Regem* 144B, 153B.
32. IG IV^2 438.
33. Roux, *L'architecture* 274: Burford, *Temple Builders* 69.
34. Kavvadias, *Arch. Eph.* 1929 198f.
35. Roux, *L'architecture* 242.
36. Roux, *L'architecture* 291.
37. *BCH* 79 (1955) 141.
38. Roux, *L'architecture* 246.
39. Compare the arrangement at the Mausoleum at Halikarnassos, the near contemporary of the Thymele, though this is rectangular, not round.
40. R. A. Tomlinson, *BSA* 64 (1969) 196f.

41. IG IV^2 40.
42. Roux, *L'architecture* 208.
43. Roux, *L'architecture* 279.
44. In his book *Gymnasium* 96.
45. Burford, *Temple Builders* 79.
46. Briefly mentioned by R. Ginouvès, *Balaneutikè* 359.
47. Burford, *Temple Builders* 75.
48. Burford, *BSA* 61 (1966) inscr. XIV, p. 296.
49. IG IV^2 104.
50. *Archaeological Reports* 1978–9 13.
51. *L'architecture* 240.

Bibliography

Burford, A., *Notes on the Epidaurian Building Inscriptions*, BSA (Annual of the British School at Athens) 61 (1966) 254–334

Burford, A., *The Greek Temple Builders of Epidauros*, Liverpool University Press, 1969

Coulton, J. J., *Greek Architects at Work*, Elek, London, 1977

Crome, J. F., *Die Skulpturen des Asklepiostempels von Epidaurus*, Berlin, 1951

Defrasse, A., and Lechat, H., *Epidaure, restauration et déscription des principaux monuments du sanctuaire d'Asclépius*, 1895

Delorme, J., *Gymnasium*, Paris, 1960

Edelstein, E. J. and L., *Asclepius*, 1945

von Gerkan, A., and Müller-Wiener, W., *Das Theater von Epidauros*, Stuttgart, 1961

Ginouvès, R., *Sur un aspect de l'évolution des bains en Grèce vers le IVe siècle de notre ère*, BCH (Bulletin de Correspondance Hellenique) 79 (1955) 141

Kavvadias, P., *Fouilles d'Epidaure*, Athens, 1891

Kavvadias, P., Τὸ ἱερόν τοῦ Ἀσκλήπιου ἐν Ἐπιδαύρῳ, Athens, 1900

Martiennsen, R., *The Idea of Space in Greek Architecture*, Witwatersrand University Press, Johannesburg, 1958

Patrucco, R., *Lo Stadio di Epidauro*, Rome, 1976

Pausanias, 'Guide to Greece' (translated by P. Levi), Penguin, 1971

Pharaklas, N., *Epidauria*, Athens

Robert, F., *Thymélè*, Paris, 1939

Roux, G., *L'architecture de l'Argolide aux IVe et IIIe siècles avant JC*, Paris, 1961

Tomlinson, R. A., *Two Buildings in Sanctuaries of Asklepios*, JHS (Journal of Hellenic Studies) 89 (1969) 106f

Index

Numerals in bold type refer to the numbered buildings in Figure 5.

97

UE